MUSEUMS OF
NEW YORK

MUSEUMS OF
NEW YORK

AN ILLUSTRATED GUIDEBOOK
TO NEW YORK'S MUSEUMS
WITH MAPS, TIME SCHEDULES,
AND RATINGS

ELOISE DANTO

ELDAN PRESS
Menlo Park, California

MUSEUMS OF NEW YORK

Copyright @ 1989 by Eloise Danto
All Rights Reserved

LIBRARY OF CONGRESS CATALOG
CARD NO. 88-083126

ISBN - 0-9615128-3-0

Printed April, 1989

Typography by Graphic Details, Palo Alto, CA

Cover Design by Michelle Taverniti, San Francisco, CA

Cover Illustrations by Christopher Grubbs, San Francisco, CA

Maps and Musuem Illustrations by Eloise Danto

Published by
ELDAN PRESS
1259 El Camino #288
Menlo Park, CA 94025

TO MARK, RACHEL, HANNAH,
ERYN, BEN AND COLLEEN

ACKNOWLEDGEMENTS

One of the happiest aspects of writing *The Museums of New York* was the contribution of time, energy, and devotion on the part of various people who donated their individual energies to the completion of this volume. To Bettina Seifert-Guerakhan, who conducted diligent research forays across Staten Island into and through its museums; to Harold Goldfarb and Stanley Disenhof, who trekked across Queens and into its museums; to Randy and Benjamin Danto, who chauffeured me across the bridges, through the tunnels, along the highways, and around the neighborhoods of New York's five boroughs; to Jayne Rattiner, who looked after me during my months of painstaking research and contributed insights and New York smarts towards the completion of my mission; to Colleen Niesen, who came through for me at the midnight hour; and to my friends and family who stood patiently in the wings while *The Museums of New York* came to fruition, I acknowledge my everlasting heartfelt thanks. Last, but not least, my thanks to you, the reader, that very special traveller, without whom Eldan Press' museum guidebook series would never have come to pass.

E.D.

INTRODUCTION

New York is one of the world's greatest art centers, the ultimate for collectors, art dealers, and, naturally, the artists who create art. New York has been accused of being glitzy, glamorous, awesome, flamboyant, intimidating, angry, and a profusion of descriptive phrases, both complimentary and unflattering. There is no denying that it possesses all these characteristics and more. New York is also one of the most exciting and complicated cities in the western world and cannot be fully appreciated without realizing the incredible number and diversity of its museums. Every mode of expression is found in one or more of New York's museums, unprecedented in scope, quality, and number of treasures; its five boroughs contain some of the most definitive collections of esoteric, experimental, alternative, and avant-garde arts found anywhere.

This astonishing city is at the center of the crossroads of multi-cultures. Its museums represent hundreds of countries and thousands of traditions. These treasure houses range from simple or primitive arts within a one-room museum to slick, sophisticated self-contained complexes, spread out across several city blocks. Some are one of a kind in the world; others might be two or three of one kind.

New York is host to 17 million out-of-towners annually. Of this number, roughly 65% are museum-goers of one degree or another. Another exciting aspect to the diversity of New York's museums is the opportunity of visiting its varied neighborhoods, from the elite Museum Mile of Fifth Avenue to the pre-Revolutionary Quaker homes in Flushing, Queens, to places of early New Amsterdam in lower Manhattan, to the patriotic Statue of Liberty/Ellis Island/ Castle Clinton triangle, and on to a surprise, Staten Island with its six museums.

Museum-going and interest in art and cultural matters is at an all time high. As a result, New York museums find themselves faced with a more responsible role.

How does a museum survive? Through membership plans tailored to fit the needs and income of its varied members; through educational programs, film series, concerts, lectures, children's programs, and organized trips; through gift shops which offer a range of gifts from 25-cent postal cards to substantial works of art for thousands of dollars; through highly polished public relations departments constantly reaching out to its clientele; and through securing the very finest in both permanent and temporary exhibitions. Within the last decade, the profession of museum management has moved into the forefront of the overall picture in the world of museums. I therefore discovered, as I visited museums, that the people who manage these temples of art from behind the scenes are fiercely dedicated to the preservation and success of their museums. Their profession then develops into an act of loving devotion, not unlike a close family community, enhancing each museum's uniqueness. Another aspect of museum management is the development of mailing lists. Within the past decade New York museums have grown to expend vast sums of money for the promotion of mail order catalogs not only for the sale of books and posters, but for faithful replicas of current exhibitions and permanent inventory. Museums which develop and maintain elaborate direct mail order programs fare much better than those which do not. In addition, the more highly developed museum shop certainly generates added income.

Not all of New York's museums are found in Manhattan. Brooklyn has seven, the Bronx seven, Staten Island six, and Washington Heights five. The remaining sixty are scattered throughout Manhattan reaching from Battery Park on up to Washington Heights at the northernmost tip of the Island of Manhattan.

New York has more Ethnic/Religious museums than any other city in the world—thirteen to be exact. They include Indian, Chinese, Japanese, Jewish, Latino, and Black. These are in addition to its historic, scientific, social, fine arts, and miscellaneous museums. If you have a particular interest or preference, there's a museum here for you. In fact, there is a museum for everyone. By the same token, there is a museum person in all of us.

Nestled in among New York's major museums are some lesser ones not to be overlooked. Some of your most intimate, rewarding visits will be realized in the smaller museums. Don't rush past any of them. There is so much good art in New York. So think carefully and consider all before discarding an idea.

The New York art audience has an insatiable taste for good art and so some of its spectacular events generate crowd crunching. Keep this in mind when attending an exhibition; it's going to be invariably good and equally crowded.

The writer gives warning to the overly enthusiastic museum-goer. Be wary of that familiar state of panic, the symptom of too much art and too much learning in too brief a time. Plan your day carefully, keeping to a certain area at one time. To avoid criss-crossing, study your local map before starting out for the day and decide on an orderly attack upon that area. Maintain a steady pace, and do not, under any circumstances, plan on doing a museum marathon, for that is a guaranteed disaster. In addition, after determining which museums you will visit, compare them with your maps of New York. You should have a street map of all five boroughs, a subway map, and an excellent map called Artwise Manhattan, all three available at book stores. Keep these with you and don't hesitate to use them. You'll save infinite time and frustration.

When planning your day's museum journey, be sure to check by telephone for the days and hours of opening. Ninety-eight percent of New York's museums are closed on Mondays. A few are open only one or two days a week. The majority of Museum Mile museums offer free entry Tuesday evenings. Most of the larger museums have fixed entry fees; others will request a suggested contribution. If you are a Senior Citizen, ID should be presented for a discount. Children are often admitted free. All this information is available in each museum's chapter.

If you are traveling with children, New York offers several special-for-kids museums. I've included these in a separate chapter under KIDS MUSEUMS. Consult the index. Two museums offer Sunday walking tours: Museum of the City of New York and the New York Historical Society. Tours meet at designated sites, charge a fee, and last from two to four hours with a lunch break. If you prefer private tours to galleries and museums, Art Tours of Manhattan takes private groups through lower New York for a charge.

The writer fervently hopes that the information presented in this simplified volume will assist you, the art traveller, in your search for the ultimate art experience. I have offered examples of what I consider to be the very best of mankind's creativity in one of my favorite cities in the western world. Even though I have barely touched upon New York's eighty museums, if I have enhanced your art adventure only slightly, it will not have been time lost. Join me now in an unusual adventure, the first of its kind, down the streets of and into those Museums of New York.

THE MUSEUMS OF NEW YORK

TABLE OF CONTENTS

LOWER MANHATTAN

1. CASTLE CLINTON NATIONAL MONUMENT
2. CITY HALL GOVERNORS ROOM
3. ELLIS ISLAND
4. FEDERAL HALL NATIONAL MOMUMENT
5. FIREFIGHTING MUSEUM
6. FRAUNCES TAVERN
7. HOLOGRAPHY MUSEUM
8. NEW MUSEUM OF CONTEMPORARY ART
9. NEW YORK STOCK EXCHANGE
10. OLD MERCHANTS HOUSE
11. SOUTH STREET SEAPORT MUSEUM
12. STATUE OF LIBERTY
13. UKRAINIAN MUSEUM

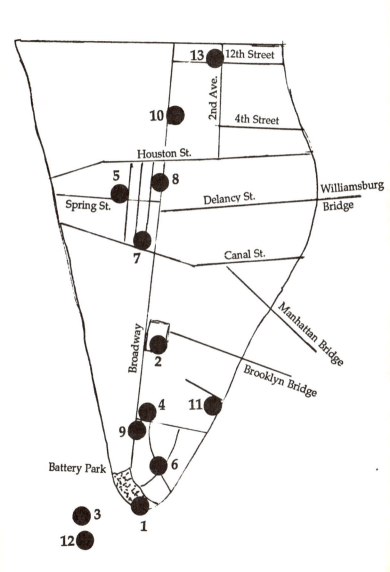

CASTLE CLINTON NATIONAL MONUMENT

OPEN:	*Daily Year Round*	ADD:	*Battery Park*
	Summer: 8-6	TEL:	*212-344-7220*
	Winter: 9-5	TYPE:	*Historical*
CLOSED:	*Christmas, New Years Day*	ENTRY:	*Free*
SUB:	*IRT #4, 5 to Bowling Green*	RATING:	**
BUS:	*M6, M15 to South Ferry*		

Here is one of New York's small museums. It's just one room, semi-circular in shape, conforming to the contour of the former fort it's in. You can't miss it: it's right in the middle of Battery Park. During the past one hundred eighty years the monument has enjoyed the tenancy of the military as a fort (1812), an entertainment center (1824), an immigration center until the creation of Ellis Island (1855), and the New York Aquarium (1930s). Drawings, lithographs, and exhibits line the walls, giving a chronological history of the monument from 1812 to the present. There's something missing here, though. Castle Clinton, together with the Statue of Liberty and Ellis Island, form a three-pronged historical museum complex. Just walk across the courtyard to buy your tickets for the ferry to the museums within the Statue.

CITY HALL GOVERNORS ROOM

OPEN: *Mon-Fri 10-2:30*	ADD: *City Hall Park*
CLOSED: *Sat, Sun, Holidays*	TEL: *212-669-4506*
SUB: *N, R, to City Hall*	TYPE: *Historical*
IRT #4, 5, 6 to Bklyn Brdg	ENTRY: *Free*
BUS: *Ml, M6 to City Hall*	RATING: ***

The City Hall building, fronted by one of New York's tiniest parks and not 50 feet away from the Brooklyn Bridge, is small and stately. It's worth coming here just to see this little gem. Once inside, walk towards the rotunda, climb the circular marble stairway, turn around, and you are there. The museum is composed of one central room and two conference chambers, all gleamingly polished. Presidential portraits by the renowned John Trumbull line the walls, along with plenty of historic memorabilia. There's Washington's writing table and some gorgeous period furnishings. This museum visit is clean, quick, and austere with a touch of dignity. After all, the mayor of New York presides in the next chamber. Then there are the quarters of the Executive Branch and the City Council of New York, all ceremoniously guarded.

ELLIS ISLAND

OPEN:	*Year-round 10-4*	ADD:	*Ellis Island*
CLOSED:	*Christmas, New Years Day*	TEL:	*212-363-3200*
FERRY:	*Year-round Daily 10-4*	TYPE:	*Historical*
	from Battery Park	ENTRY:	*Free*
	Every hour	RATING:	***
	Adult $3, Sr & Stud $2		

In 1890, construction was begun on Ellis Island as a receiving/ processing immigration center in New York Harbor. Between 1892 and 1954, a mere 62 years, almost 17 million people entered the United States, the largest human migration in modern history. Over the years the complex and its facilities deteriorated and in 1964 work was begun to restore the waiting rooms, dormitories, hospital, telegraph station, train ticketing office, kitchens, dining rooms, and, of course, the imposing Great Room, where the official museum is now located. It's eclectic with the original atmosphere of anxious drama. For a $100 donation one can honor any immigrant ancestor of any nationality with a plaque placed on the Wall of Honor in the museum. For that matter, any individual or family name can be placed there. Welcome back, Ellis Island.

FEDERAL HALL NATIONAL MONUMENT

OPEN: *Mon-Fri 9-5*
CLOSED: *Sat, Sun, all Holidays*
except Washington's
B'day and July 4
SUB: *IRT #2, 3, 4 to Wall St*
BUS: *Ml, M6, Ml5 to*
South Ferry

ADD: *26 Wall St @ Nassau St*
TEL: *212-264-8711*
TYPE: *Historical*
ENTRY: *Free*
RATING: ***

The building was constructed in 1699 and is one of New York's oldest. Originally it was the City Hall, then a Customs House, and thereafter was constantly used as one Federal agency or another. It enjoys distinction as the site of George Washington's innauguration in 1789. The museum upstairs holds cabinets and cases filled with Washingtonia as well as all sorts of information about the Republic, the Revolutionary War, and the first constitutional government of the United States. In the early years of our nation, New York City was the nation's capital and was beset with the not unusual urban problems of water pollution, the need for parks, and raising money by means of a lottery. George Washington dominates the entire atmosphere; he presides outside the building in stately bronze.

FIREFIGHTING MUSEUM

OPEN:	*Tues-Sat 10-4*	ADD:	*278 Spring St*
CLOSED:	*Sun, Mon*	TEL:	*212-691-1303*
SUB:	*IND C, E, K to Spring St*	TYPE:	*Miscellaneous*
BUS:	*M6, M8, M10 to*	ENTRY:	*Voluntary Donation*
	Spring St	RATING:	***

Does your pulse race when you hear the roar of a fire
engine? Ever wonder why the Dalmatian is the mascot of
fire houses? Well, don't miss this museum. It's a former fire
house three stories high, with bright red doors. The
collection on the main floor presents firefighting memorabilia and traces the history of firefighting with vehicles,
equipment, and fire trucks. The second floor captures the
tradition and pageantry of early firefighting, and presents
an exhibit on some of New York's spectacular fires. There's
a library containing records and files, photographs of
engines, and portraits of fire officials. This museum is
particulary appealing to children and school groups, not
only for its fire prevention program, but for its vivid
portrayal of firefighting pride and the powerful, uncanny
camaraderie among firefighters.

FRAUNCES TAVERN

OPEN:	*Mon-Fri 10-4*	ADD:	*54 Pearl St @ B'way*
	Sun 12-4	TEL:	*212-425-1776*
CLOSED:	*Sat & Holidays*	TYPE:	*Historical*
SUB:	*IND R, N to*	ENTRY:	*Adult $2.50*
	Whitehall St		*Sr & Stud $1*
BUS:	*M1, M6 to South Ferry*	RATING:	***

There really was a Sam Fraunces. He was the West Indian steward of George Washington who bought this building and turned it into a tavern, which became a popular gathering place for prominent citizens of early New York. At the turn of the 20th century it was restored and preserved as a museum. It's one flight up and is composed of three rooms which focus on the history and culture of New York at the time of the Revolutionary War, plus the room where George Washington bid his historic farewell to his officers. Documents, drawings, and lithographs line the walls, and period furnishings are placed about. The museum is beautifully maintained in meticulous detail, appearing as it did 200 years ago. Workshops, concerts and theatrical performances are hosted hers. There's a tiny gift shop, and the small restaurant downstairs has an excellent menu for either lunch or dinner.

MUSEUM OF HOLOGRAPHY

OPEN:	*Tues-Sun ll-6*	ADD:	*ll Mercer St*
CLOSED:	*Mon*	TEL:	*212-925-0526*
SUB:	*Lex Ave #6*	TYPE:	*Miscellaneous*
	to Canal St	ENTRY:	*Adult $3*
			Sr & Stud $2.75
		RATING:	*

Holography is a uniquely creative new art form invented here in the 1940s, and it is neither widely understood nor fully appreciated. Simply put, it's the exposure of photographic film to a laser beam which creates a three-dimensional image. The effect is somewhat eerie, for the image transforms as the viewer moves about in various positions in front of the art, thus changing the effect by distance and angle. Colors are brilliant, and no two holograms are alike. The main floor of this museum has an assortment of holograms varying in size from a few inches to several feet. Downstairs there is a small theatre for a permanent exhibit and a small theater for video films on the principle of holography. Unfortunately, the museum, despite the appeal of its subject, is dusty and shabby, and it needs either refurbishing, a facelift, or both.

NEW MUSEUM OF CONTEMPORARY ART

OPEN:	*Wed, Thurs, Sun 12-6*	ADD:	*583 B'way @ Spring*
	Fri 12-10 , Sat 12-8	TEL:	*212-219-1222*
CLOSED:	*Mon, Tues & Holidays*	TYPE:	*Fine Arts*
SUB:	*IRT #6 to Spring St*	ENTRY:	*Adult $2.50*
BUS:	*5th Ave #1 to*		*Sr & Stud $1.50*
	B'way & Houston	RATING:	***

This museum is relatively unknown and may not be listed
in all guidebooks. It's located in the Soho district, which,
when translated, means South of Houston (Street), since
1983. Innovative contemporary collections are shown on a
rotating basis. The main perequisite for an artist to exhibit
is that he or she must be alive and have created their
contemporary art within the past ten years. Several major
exhibitions originate here each year, some offbeat, others
eclectic, all exciting. The museum publishes its own art
related books. Their library, called the Soho Center Library
for Contemporary Art, is open to critics, scholars, art
professionals, and art aficionados. This is a serious,
intelligent museum: small but good, with sparkling pres-
ence. I would recommend checking it out.

NEW YORK STOCK EXCHANGE

OPEN:	*Mon-Fri 10-4*	
CLOSED:	*Sat, Sun & Holidays*	
SUB:	*7th Ave #2, 3 to Wall St*	

ADD:	*20 Broad St @ Wall St*
TEL:	*212-656-5167*
TYPE:	*Miscellaneous*
ENTRY:	*Free*
RATING:	***

How many times have you been to New York and never entertained the notion of visiting the Stock Exchange? Well, get in line for the 10 a.m. opening, take the elevator upstairs, and move through several rooms to the glass-enclosed balcony overlooking the trading floor. It's pure pandemonium and difficult to believe that those scurrying figures below know what they're doing and where they're going, assuming they do. You'll learn quite a bit about trading, international financial matters, and the system of those red electronic numbers flashing across the walls. A six-minute film explains the fundamentals and mechanics of the Market. There are seven Stock Exchanges across the US. This one is the largest and the only one permitting visitors. And believe it or not, you can buy a NYSE tee shirt at the gift shop.

OLD MERCHANTS HOUSE

OPEN:	*Sunday 1-4*	ADD:	*29 E. 4th St*
CLOSED:	*August, All Holidays*	TEL:	*212-777-1089*
SUB:	*IRT Lex #6 to Astor Pl*	TYPE:	*Historical*
	IND A, B, D, E, F	ENTRY:	*Adult $2*
	to 4th St		*Sr & Stud $1*
		RATING:	***

The Old Merchants House is a rare treasure built in 1832 and
recently restored. With the exception of the draperies and
carpeting, all furnishings are original and still glistening.
The house truly reflects the fashionable life-style of a
prosperous New York family, laden with heavy Victori-
ana—from Greek Revival parlors to Gothic Revival bed
chambers—and if you peek into the closets you'll find
handsome period clothing and accessories. Intimate family
memorabilia are sprinkled about. The kitchen was appar-
ently the center of family activities with its cast iron stove,
brick oven, and sink with a hand pump. There's an aura of
privacy throughout the entire house, almost as though
someone from this family might suddenly appear, offended
by our intrusion.

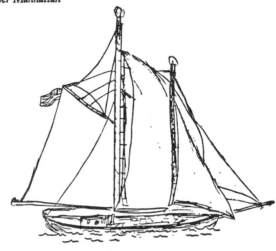

SOUTH STREET SEAPORT MUSEUM

OPEN:	*Daily Year-Round 10-5*	**ADD:**	*East River @ Fulton St*
		TEL:	*212-669-9424*
SUB:	*IRT #2, 3 to Fulton St*	**TYPE:**	*Historical*
	Lex #4, 5 to Fulton St	**ENTRY:**	*Museum-Adult $5*
BUS:	*2nd Ave to Fulton St*		*Sr & Stud $3*
		RATING:	***

There really is a museum, just look for it on John Street at
the River. It has ship models, maritime paintings and
memorabilia of ocean liners. But it's the seaport area that
draws the crowds. The complex is spread out across a half-
mile under the Brooklyn Bridge with trendy shops, bou-
tiques, and eateries, and at the river's edge there are several
tall ships and sailboats, boardable and sailable for a New
York harbor cruise. Be prepared for crowds with high
energy levels and stores with prices to match. In 1820,
Robert Fulton started a ferry service from here to Brooklyn,
put his name on a street and a fish market, and the rest is
history. If you can get past the din, South Street Seaport is a
fun try at the remembrance of an historic district of Old
New York.

STATUE OF LIBERTY

OPEN:	*Daily Year-Round 10-4*	ADD:	*Liberty Island*
CLOSED:	*Christmas, N.Years Day*	TEL:	*212-363-3200*
FERRY:	*From Battery Park,*	TYPE:	*Historical*
	daily every hour on	ENTRY:	*All $1*
	the hour 9-4.	RATING:	****
	Tickets: Adult $3		
	Sr & Stud $2		

Aside from the Mona Lisa in Paris, Liberty is surely one of the most celebrated women in the world, a stirring sight majestically rising out of New York harbor. Thanks to French sculptor F. A. Bartholdi and Gustave Eiffel, designer of the Eiffel Tower in Paris, plus hundreds of craftsmen and thousands of contributors from many nations, she is the symbol of friendship, liberty, compassion, and courage. In 1986 for her 100th birthday and America's Centennial, her radiant luster was gloriously restored. There are two museums within the Statue. The first, the Museum of the Statue, recounts the history of her creation. The second, the Immigration Museum, is dedicated to the history of US immigration. Be prepared for long lines unless you arrive early. If you're up to it, a climb of 22 stories will bring you to her crown for a panoramic view of New York harbor.

UKRAINIAN MUSEUM

OPEN: *Wed-Sun 1-5*	ADD: *203 Second Ave @ 12 St*
CLOSED: *Mon, Tues, Thanksgiving,*	TEL: *212-228-0110*
Christmas,	TYPE: *Ethnic*
New Years Day	ENTRY: *Adult $3*
SUB: *IRT Lex #4, 5, 6 to 14 St*	*Sr & Stud $2*
at Union Square	RATING: *****

The Ukraine is a country in the southwestern corner of the
Soviet Union bordering on the Black Sea, Poland and
Rumania. This museum, brimming with ethnicity, occupies
the fourth and fifth floors of a renovated brownstone. Its
collections are folk art crafts from the 19th and 20th centuries. Ukrainian history is chronicled through photos,
drawings, and costume displays. There's a case of intricately
painted eggs. You must have seen them at one time or
another and may not have realized their origin. They're
traditional folk art symbols of fertility and spring rites.
Classes are given for egg painting, embroidery, bead
stringing, and holiday decorations. The museum, an
important center for the Ukrainian community, devotes
itself to the perpetuation of public awareness of their
relatively unknown culture.

MURRAY HILL

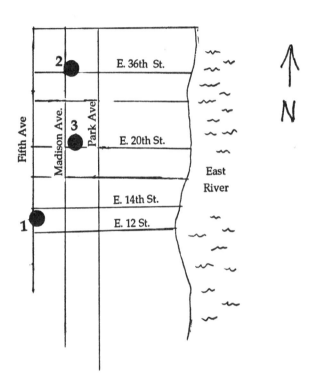

1. FORBES MAGAZINE GALLERY
2. PIERREPONT MORGON LIBRARY
3. THEODORE ROOSEVELT BIRTHPLACE

FORBES MAGAZINE GALLERIES

OPEN:	*Tues-Sat 10-4*	ADD:	*62 5th Ave @ 12 St*
CLOSED:	*Sun, Mon, Holidays*	TEL:	*212-206-5548*
SUB:	*IRT #1, 2, 3 to 14 St*	TYPE:	*Gallery*
BUS:	*M1, M2, M3 to 14 St*	ENTRY:	*Free*
		RATING:	****

The galleries, located on the ground floor of the Forbes Building, are the private collection of the legendary Forbes family. Once inside, your course has been plotted out for you. Simply follow the arrows. Begin with Ships Ahoy, eight gold glass panels of ship fittings plus a century of toy boats. Next is On Parade, a corps of toy armies and miniature lead soldiers portraying glorious battles of past centuries. Next is the Trophies Gallery, a collection of awards from world-wide teams, groups, and individuals. Then on to Presidential Papers for personal letters, documents, and drawings of American Presidents. Following is Faberge, the dazzling collection of eggs, objects of art, and jewelled treasures of the Czars. In addition there are four historic Miniature Rooms. Top this off with the Fine Arts Gallery, which holds exquisite paintings of the Masters, the envy of any museum, and you've had a gorgeous museum visit.

PIERREPONT MORGAN LIBRARY

OPEN: *Tues-Sat 10:30-5, Sun 1-5*	ADD: *29 E 36 St @ Madison*
CLOSED: *Mon & Holidays*	TEL: *212-685-0008*
SUB: *IND E, F to 34 St*	TYPE: *General*
BUS: *M1, M2, M3, M4*	ENTRY: *Suggested Adult $3*
to 34 St	*Sr & Stud $1*
	RATING: ****

The library was built for Mr. Morgan at the beginning of this
century. Its purpose is twofold. First, it is a center for
scholarly research. Second, it is one of New York's most
distinguished museums. Mr. Morgan was a rich, crusty, and
powerful philanthropist with consuming interests in music,
literature, the arts, history, and an elegant life style. His
collections of Old Master drawings, sculptures, illuminated
medieval and Renaissance manuscripts, musical manuscripts, early printed books and bindings, and first edition
children's books, are among the finest in the world. His
study is a museum in itself, with paneled ceilings, rich wood
walls, paintings, and massive furnishings. The Library
exhibits drawings, autographed manuscripts, and rare
books drawn from Mr. Morgan's private collection. This is a
virtual treasure of culture.

THEODORE ROOSEVELT BIRTHPLACE

OPEN:	*Wed-Sun 9-5*	ADD:	*28 E 20 St*
CLOSED:	*Mon, Tues, Major Hol.*	TEL:	*212-260-1616*
SUB:	*IRT #6 to 23 St*	TYPE:	*Historical*
BUS:	*M1, M2, M3 to*	ENTRY:	*Adult $1*
	Park Ave & 21 St		*Sr & Stud Free*
		RATING:	*****

This brownstone witnessed the birth and formative years of TR, frail, fragile, and asthmatic until, at the age of 12, he commenced rigorous training and developed into a robust, aggressive young man, becoming passionately involved with the Museum of Natural History. He published essays and books on natural history and public affairs, took expeditions to Africa and South America, created some of our national parks and game preserves, and hunted big game. He was a rancher and cowboy, galloping with and heading the Rough Riders. He was Governor of New York, President of the US, Nobel Peace Prize winner, and more. The museum has been restored beautifully to its original dignified grace and Victorian high fashion. Some furnishings are original and all rooms are bursting with Teddy memorabilia. There's a small Teddy Bear in a showcase. Here was a home filled with much love and extraordinary family devotion which still prevails.

MIDTOWN EAST

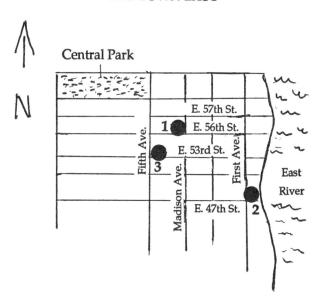

1. IBM GALLERY
2. JAPAN SOCIETY
3. MUSUEM OF BROADCASTING

IBM GALLERY OF SCIENCE AND ART

OPEN:	*Tues-Fri 11-6*	ADD:	*IBM Bldg*
	Sat 10-5		*Madison Ave @ 56 St*
CLOSED:	*Sun, Mon*	TEL:	*212-407-6100*
SUB:	*IND E, F to 5th Ave*	TYPE:	*Gallery*
BUS:	*M1, M2, M3,*	ENTRY:	*Free*
	M4 to 57 St	RATING:	******

To begin with, IBM has been more than generous in its
support of the arts since its founding in the 1930s. The
reason I've included it in this museum book is that it ranks
as high as some museums in its significant range of exhibitions in science and art. All shows are temporary, each
remaining approximately two months. The downstairs
auditorium runs continuous art-related films. Because of
the high quality of its exhibitions of Folk Art, US Indian Art,
Japanese woodblock, IBM's own collections, scientific
exhibitions, computers, and art shows, the IBM Gallery rates
as an important art center in New York and should be
visited. It's also one of the best in manner of presentation,
level of professionalism, and quality of exhibitions. And it's
all free.

JAPAN SOCIETY

OPEN:	*Tues-Sun 11-5*	ADD:	*333 E 47 St @ 1st Ave*
CLOSED:	*Monday*	TEL:	*212-752-0824*
SUB:	*IRT #6 to 51 St*	TYPE:	*Ethnic*
BUS:	*M 15, M 27 to 47 St*	ENTRY:	*Free*
		RATING:	***

This building of authentic modern Japanese design is the only one of its kind in New York. Located directly across from the UN, the Society attracts a large Asian following. On entering, you'll see a reflecting pool from which small bamboo trees rise. Maryell Semal, the museum's Assistant Director, sat with me in a cool, high-ceilinged room which looked out into a serene inner courtyard and spoke of the purpose of the Society: it cultivates and enhances the Japan/US relationship in a cultural, artistic, intellectual, and political sense. Music festivals, folk ballets, and tours to Japan are ongoing. Lectures on international business are held for both the American and Japanese communities. Japan Society proves that an intelligent venture of two diametrically opposite cultures can successfully flourish.

MUSEUM OF BROADCASTING

OPEN:	*Wed-Sat 12-5*	ADD:	*1 East 53 St*
	Tues 12-8	TEL:	*212-752-4690*
CLOSED:	*Sun, Mon*	TYPE:	*Media*
SUB:	*IRT Lex Ave #4, 5, 6*	ENTRY:	*Suggested Donation*
	to 51 St		*Adult $4*
BUS:	*5th Ave to 53 St*		*Sr & Stud $3*
		RATING:	****

This brand-new museum is really a mammoth archive of
digital tapes of radio and TV programming and advertise-
ments from 1920 to the present, crammed full of old favorites.
Every major public event ever filmed is available for your
individual screening. Go on up to the 4th floor library and
select your program from the computer-generated catalog.
You will be given your own console. Just to mention a few
tapes: Edward R. Morrow's "This is London", FDR's fireside
chats, early Beatles, space shots, moon landings, Sid Caesar,
Ernie Kovacs, wartime newsreels, and more. Retrospectives
are shown in the main floor theater. The vast microfiche
library contains a myriad of radio scripts. Saturday screen-
ings for kids, too. This museum enjoys great attendance.
Future plans involve a move to larger quarters on 52 St.
What a fun adventure for all!

MIDTOWN WEST

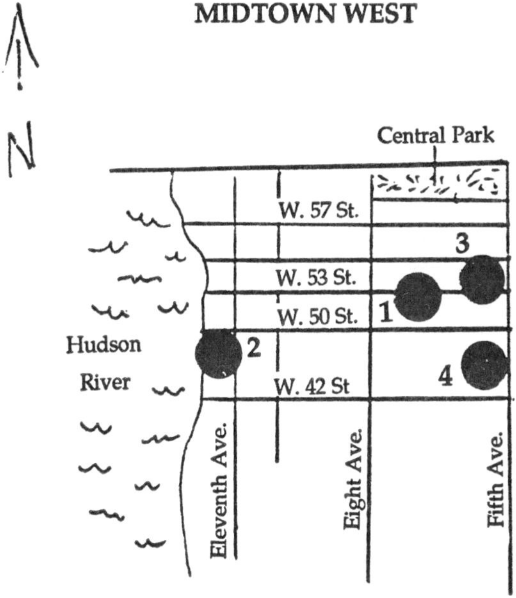

1. AMERICAN CRAFT MUSUEM
2. INTREPID
3. MUSUEM OF MODERN ART
4. NY PUBLIC LIBRARY

AMERICAN CRAFT MUSEUM

OPEN:	*Tues 10-8*	ADD:	*40 West 53 St*
	Wed-Sun 10-5	TEL:	*956-6047*
CLOSED:	*Mon & Holidays*	TYPE:	*Fine Arts*
SUB:	*IND E, F to Fifth Ave*	ENTRY:	*Adult $3.50*
BUS:	*M1, M2, M3 to 53 St*		*Sr & Stud $1.50*
			Tues Evening Free
		RATING:	****

The American Craft Council maintains a role of leadership
in the US craft movement and here is the premiere showcase
for their craft forms, both traditional and innovative, with
accent on the latter. Thanks to the Council, crafts have
come to be recognized as a major force in the panoramic
placement of art. An eclectic component of this museum is
its atrium and central stairway, which give sweeping
visibility to four levels of the unique art form currently
appearing. Shows present architecture, furnishings,
sculpture, ceramics, glass, fiber, wood and metal, plus many
additional media categories, all of particular originality and
lovingly displayed. Each visit by the writer revealed
exceptional talent. On the lowest level there's a playroom
center with ingenious art games, inviting all to participate.
Please create your own art. What an exciting visit!

INTREPID

OPEN: *Wed-Sun 10-5*	ADD: *W. 46 St @ Hudson River*
CLOSED: *Mon, Tues, Winter Hol*	TEL: *212-245-2533*
SUB: *All lines to 42 St,*	TYPE: *Miscellaneous*
Crosstown M42	ENTRY: *Adult $4.75*
BUS: *M42 to Carrier*	*Sr & Stud $4*
	RATING: ***

The heroic carrier Intrepid opened her doors as the Sea-Air-Space Museum in 1981. She is more than impressive, she's downright patriotic. Here is a presentation of naval might and heroism in war with larger-than-life photos, exhibits, and aircraft from Kitty Hawk on up to Vietnam. What American is not thrilled by aircraft parked on the Flight Deck, the Combat Information Center, the Hangar Deck with exhibit halls presenting nothing less than sheer adventure, plus a movie theater with thrilling footage of carrier takeoffs, landings and flight operations accompanied by great sound effects from radio's war years, 1940s music, and voices of Intrepid's crew during combat situations. If you've ever wondered about the tension on board a carrier, stand at one end of the deck and look down its length. Visualize taking off or landing a jet while moving across a rolling sea at about 35 miles an hour.

MUSEUM OF MODERN ART

OPEN:	*Fri-Tues ll-6, Thurs ll-9*	ADD:	*ll West 53 St @ 5th Ave*
CLOSED:	*Wed*	TEL:	*212-708-9480*
SUB:	*IND E, F to 5th Ave & 53 St*	TYPE:	*Fine Arts*
		ENTRY:	*Adult $5*
BUS:	*Ml, M2, M3, M4 to 52 St*		*Sr & Stud $3.50*
		RATING:	******

MOMA is at the top of the list with its white marble and glass facade and unrivalled collection of all Modern Art movements from the l9th century to the present. In addition to its superb painting and sculpture galleries, there are architectural, industrial, and graphic design collections, cinema, furniture and photography collections, drawings and prints, all are the creme de la creme. Artists shown are Rodin, Calder, Moore, Gaugin, Van Gogh, Pollack, and Redon, to name just a few. Two downstairs theaters offer free films and lectures. Since one side of the museum is a wall of glass, the interior light is exquisite. Of course, visit the Sculpture Garden with its abundance of sitting space and exquisite fountains, sculptures, then go on to the Garden Cafe for a snack. The two-leveled museum store carries an enormous selection of books and gifts. MOMA is not just a museum, it's a consummate repository of 20th-century art.

NEW YORK PUBLIC LIBRARY

OPEN:	*Mon, Wed 10-8:45*	ADD:	*5th Ave @ 42 St*
	Tues, Thurs, Sat 10- 5:45	TEL:	*212-930-0800*
CLOSED:	*Sunday*	TYPE:	*General*
SUB:	*IRT #7 to 42 St*	ENTRY:	*Free*
	IND D to 42 St	RATING:	****
BUS:	*M1, M2, M3, M4 to 42 St*		

Climb up the broad steps under the watchful eyes of
Patience and Fortitude, the two majestic lions guarding the
entrance. This is not only a place where one would borrow
one of eight million books, return it, and continue borrow-
ing forever, but it's the main branch of a system that covers
New York's five boroughs with more than eighty branches.
This immense Beaux Arts building contains a wealth of
archives whose scope defies the imagination, but includes
rare books and manuscripts, illustrations, prints, engravings
and paintings. Its Great Reading Room alone is larger than
most libraries. There are three floors, each bursting with
galleries of learning. Do stop at the Celeste Bartos Forum, a
gorgeous salon for lectures, concerts, and films. This is the
only place I know of where one can secure a complete
education absolutely free.

UPTOWN EAST

1. ABIGAIL ADAMS SMITH
2. ASIA SOCIETY
3. CENTER FOR AFRICAN ART
4. CENTRAL PARK ZOO
5. CHINA INSTITUTE
6. COOPER-HEWITT (SMITHSONIAN)
7. EL MUSEO DEL BARRIO
8. FRICK COLLECTION
9. GUGGENHEIM MUSEUM
10. INTERNATIONAL CENTER OF PHOTOGRAPH
11. JEWISH MUSEUM
12. METROPOLITAN MUSEUM OF ART
13. MUSEUM OF THE CITY OF NEW YORK
14. NATIONAL ACADEMY OF DESIGN
15. UKRAINIAN INSTITUTE
16. WHITNEY MUSEUM

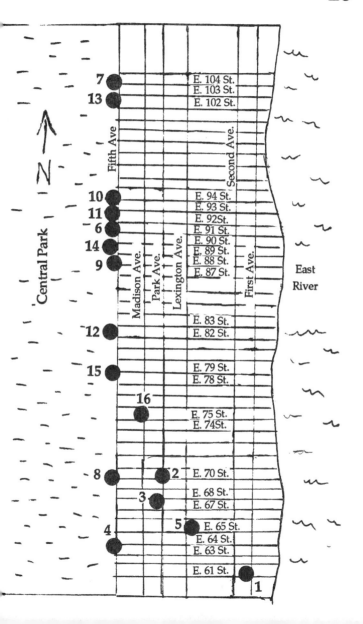

ABIGAIL ADAMS SMITH

OPEN: *Mon-Fri 10-4*	ADD: *421 E 61 St @ 2nd Ave*
CLOSED: *Sat, Sun, Aug & Hol*	TEL: *838-6878*
SUB: *Lex IRT to 59 St*	TYPE: *Historical*
BUS: *3rd Ave to 61 St*	ENTRY: *Adult $3 Sr & Stud $1*
	RATING: **

Abigail Adams Smith was the daughter of John Adams and the sister of John Quincy Adams. Picture her nine-room stone carriage house, built in 1799 and now under the shadow of the Queensboro Bridge, surrounded by New York's East Side's clatter and clutter. It's a secluded gem filled with original furnishings, arts and memorabilia from the late 18th century: a charming colonial kitchen, a spinning wheel, and just plain simple, elegant decor. The quaint house is one of those rare handful of buildings in New York which have survived from the 18th century. Thanks to some tender loving care on the part of the Colonial Dames of America, who maintain and escort tours through the house, its quaintness endures. Odd, isn't it, that Abigail Adams Smith never lived here? During summer months the museum remains open until 8 p.m. for concerts in the tranquil gardens. $3 admission. Refreshments will be served.

ASIA SOCIETY GALLERY

OPEN: *Tues-Sat 10-6, Sun 12-5*	ADD: *725 Park Ave*
CLOSED: *Mon*	TEL: *212-288-6400*
SUB: *IRT Lex 3, 4 to 68 St*	TYPE: *Ethnic*
BUS: *2nd Ave to 70 St*	ENTRY: *Adult $2*
	Sr & Stud $1
	RATING: ***

The Asia Society building, in striking contrast to its Park Avenue apartment house neighborhood, is of two-tone red granite with clean lines. Its purpose is twofold. First, it houses the Society's offices and visiting exhibitions, and second, it displays the private and permanent collection of the John D. Rockefellers, which is the core of what's here, and handsome it is. Mr. Rockefeller, an astute collector, gathered these Asian treasures with loving devotion, and in the process achieved total perfection. Eminent speakers appear, photographic exhibits and Asian films are shown, and dance performances are regularly given in the lower level theater. After you've seen the gallery, allow yourself a few extra moments to visit the terrace with its graceful and soothing fountains. Then it's back to the outside world.

CENTER FOR AFRICAN ART

OPEN: *Tues-Fri 10-5*	ADD: *54 E 68 St*
Sat 11-5	TEL: *212-861-1200*
Sun 12-5	TYPE: *Ethnic*
CLOSED: *Mon & Holidays*	ENTRY: *Voluntary Contribution*
SUB: *IRT Lex to 68 St*	RATING: **
BUS: *Lex Ave to 65 St*	

The museum is housed in a small Victorian mansion, unusual for New York's upper East Side. When the Museum of Primitive Art merged into the Rockefeller Wing of the Metropolitan, New York was left without a center for African art. Now, this brand new Center has been redesigned and dedicated to increasing the understanding and appreciation of Africa's ancient cultures through well-researched, well-planned, and well-executed presentations. The interior, updated to accommodate their specific needs, is nicely done. Three exhibitions a year are held, for which the Center publishes its own catalogs and brochures. It also sponsors related lectures, slide shows and film programs. Books on African Art are sold on the main floor. If the current shows are any indication of this small museum's quality, it is guaranteed to be a success.

CENTRAL PARK ZOO

OPEN:	*Year-round Mon-Fri 10-5*	ADD:	*5th Ave @ 64 St*
	Sat, Sun, Hol 10-5:30	TEL:	*212-360-8213*
	Tues Eves 10-8	TYPE:	*Zoological*
	(summer only)	ENTRY:	*Adult $1*
SUB:	*IRT Lex to 68 St*		*Sr & Stud .50*
BUS:	*Madison Ave to 64 St*	RATING:	****

You must admit that finding a zoo in the middle of New York City is rather unusual. This is a brand new one, and thanks to the New York Zoological Society the scene of action proves that you don't need to be big to be good. The zoo is divided into ten different areas and three major climate zones: tropical, temperate, and polar. Appropriate animals are placed within their respective sectors. Walk leisurely through the animals' naturalistic environments, up and around the landscape of the park. It's a beautifully designed setting, from its elegant arcade and central garden down to the sea lion pool. Break up the day with a light lunch in the garden cafe. The Children's Zoo, just next door, is an extra treat at only 10 cents admission for all.

CHINA INSTITUTE IN AMERICA

OPEN:	*Mon-Fri 10-5*	ADD:	*125 E 65 St*
	Sat 11-5	TEL:	*212-744-8181*
	Sun 2-5	TYPE:	*Ethnic*
SUB:	*IRT Lex to 68 St*	ENTRY:	*Donations accepted*
BUS:	*2nd Ave to 63 St*	RATING:	***
	3rd Ave to 63 St		

The museum is called The China House Gallery. It's set in one room of a townhouse of the China Institute, its parent organization. The Institute is a pioneering promoter of the US-China relationship via art, painting, film series, and history and language classes, and has advanced America's knowledge and appreciation of China's fascinating history and culture. It also succeeds in providing support groups and career building services to the Chinese-American community. Tours to Japan, China, and Thailand are offered, and the School of Chinese Studies is well attended. There are two principal shows held yearly; each is devoted exclusively to Chinese Art. After your tour of the Gallery, walk through the Institute for some first-hand insights into celebrating a culture thousands of years old.

COOPER-HEWITT MUSEUM (SMITHSONIAN)

OPEN:	*Wed-Sat 10-5*	ADD:	*2 E 91 St*
	Tues 10-9	TEL:	*212-860-6868*
	Sun 12-5	TYPE:	*Fine Arts*
CLOSED:	*Mon & Holidays*	ENTRY:	*Adult $3*
SUB:	*IRT Lex to 86 St*		*Sr & Stud $1.50*
BUS:	*5th or Mad to 86 St*		*Free Tues 5-9*
		RATING:	****

Millionaire Andrew Carnegie had this 64-room mansion
custom built in 1901, lived in it with his family, and conducted his business affairs here. To say that it's elegant is
an understatement. It's spacious, baronial and comfortable.
But what better setting for the likes of this museum, an
important center for Decorative Arts and the design process
of cities, landscapes, theater, the arts and architecture, glass,
and ceramics. Its galleries cover designs for every historical
period over a span of 3,000 years. The museum was
dormant for a number of years but is now enjoying a
renaissance. The changing exhibitions really give Cooper
Hewitt its magnetism; all are excellent, and why not—,it's
part of the Smithsonian. The library alone is worth the visit.
There is an enormous amount of dynamic energy throughout, and it's absolute heaven.

EL MUSEO DEL BARRIO

OPEN:	*Wed-Sun 11-5*	ADD:	*1230 5th Ave @ 104 St*
CLOSED:	*Mon, Tues*	TEL:	*212-831-7272*
SUB:	*IRT Lex to 103 St*	TYPE:	*Ethnic*
BUS:	*Mad Ave to 104 St*	ENTRY:	*Voluntary Donation*
		RATING:	***

This is the only museum in the country dedicated to the arts and culture of Puerto Rico, South and Central America, and the Caribbean. It's also a distinguished Latin American cultural institution. It was organized in 1969 by a group of Puerto Rican parents to bring to their people a sense of Latino ancestry through the arts. They have succeeded. The Hispanic community in New York has responded over-whelmingly. Not only have artists, writers, sculptors and film- makers respectfully submitted their works for viewing, but Latinos from all parts of New York now gravitate towards this Center for Latin American folk music, concerts, festivals, competitions and changing exhibitions, lectures, and public education classes. The organizers and their entire community deserve kudos for enduring determination.

FRICK COLLECTION

OPEN: *Tues-Sat 10-6*	ADD: *1 E. 70 St @ 5th Ave*
Sun, Feb 12, Nov 11 1-6	TEL: *212-288-0700*
CLOSED: *Mon, N. Years Day, July 4,*	TYPE: *Fine Arts*
Thanksgiving, Christmas	ENTRY: *Adult $3*
SUB: *IRT Lex #6 to 68 St*	RATING: ****
BUS: *M1, M2, M3, M4 to 68 St*	

As its name implies, this was the home of the Frick family.
It's where they lived, worked, and entertained. To give
some light on the background of this mansion, Henry Frick
was a notorious, swashbuckling industrialist billionaire with
exceptionally good taste in the fine arts. It was he who
amassed this spectacular collection of breathtaking artistry.
If you're curious about his appearance, his portrait hangs in
the library over the fireplace. But it's not only the works of
art that lend the feeling of sensuality here, it's the decorative
arts surrounding them—the walls, ceilings, carpets, and
other accoutrements. The inner courtyard with its delicate
fountains completes the sensation of total gratification. The
Frick is a major museum attraction in New York. It will take
your breath away. Don't miss it.

GUGGENHEIM MUSEUM

OPEN:	*Wed-Sun 11-5*	ADD:	*1071 5th Ave @ 88 St*
	Tues 11-8	TEL:	*212-360-3500*
CLOSED:	*Mon, Christmas*	TYPE:	*Fine Arts*
SUB:	*IRT Lex to 86 St*	ENTRY:	*Adult $3.50*
BUS:	*Mad Ave to 86 St*		*Sr & Stud $2*
			Free Tues Eve 5-8
		RATING:	****

By now you know not only that Frank Loyd Wright
designed this building, but that it's his only work in New
York City. And it's not only what's being shown here, but
what it's being shown in that draws huge crowds. Alas, Mr.
Wright did not live to see its opening in 1939. The museum
owns about 180 canvasses of Kandinsky, scores of Chagalls,
and numerous works by Impressionists, Post-Impression-
ists, the School of Paris, etc., and there are more Cezannes
here than in Paris. At Mr. Wright's suggestion, visitors start
at the top of the museum and descend its seven floors to the
circular main floor below. The museum shop has some of
the most exciting gifts in any museum, including eclectic
jewelry and small Calder mobiles. You don't have to be a
fan of Modern Art to love the Guggenheim—just relax and
enjoy the show.

INTERNATIONAL CENTER OF PHOTOGRAPHY

OPEN:	*Wed-Fri 12-5*	ADD:	*1130 5th Ave @ 94 St*
	Sat, Sun 11-6	TEL:	*212-860-1777*
	Tues 12-8	TYPE:	*Media*
CLOSED:	*Mon & Holidays*	ENTRY:	*Adult $2.50*
SUB:	*IRT Lex to 96 St*		*Sr & Stud $1*
BUS:	*Mad Ave to 96 St*		*Free Tues Eves 5-8*
		RATING:	****

The museum is devoted exclusively to the technique and
style of photographers and photography. Collections,
programs and publications embrace the universe of the
camera. Exhibiting participants exemplify camera artistry
through landscapes, still lifes, portraits and figures, and the
viewer is bestowed with an aura of privilege. Galleries
contain extraordinary photography, and the list of master
craftsmen of photojournalism is more than impressive:
Capa, White, Cartier-Bresson, Feininger, Atget, Arbus,
Steiglitz, Weston, all here in imposing grandeur. Aside
from lecture series and workshops, accredited Master-of-
Arts programs are offered. The basement is occupied by
darkrooms, finishing rooms, a gallery for attending students
and a screening room. If you're searching for a thrilling
museum, ICP is for you. Ah, the power of the picture.

JEWISH MUSEUM

OPEN: *Mon, Wed, Thurs 12-5*	ADD: *5th Ave @ 92 St*
Tues 12-8 , Sun 11-6	TEL: *212-860-1885*
CLOSED: *Fri, Sat, Jewish Hol*	TYPE: *Ethnic*
SUB: *IRT Lex to 96 St*	ENTRY: *Adult $4, Sr & Stud $2*
BUS: *Mad Ave to 92 St*	*Free Tues Eves 5-8*
	RATING: ****

The museum is under the auspices of the Jewish Theological Seminary of America and dedicates itself to illuminating Jewish art, culture and tradition through arts, artifacts and ceremonial objects and the expression of Jewish identity. Israeli artists are prevalent but Jewish artists from other countries are given equal space. Much of the collection was taken from pre-WW II synagogues of Europe, when far-sighted Jewry realized that, in order to preserve their legacy, they had better move their precious objects out of Europe to the U.S. The archeological display gives glowing light into Israel's 4,000 year history. The tiny five-seat theatre in the corner of one room shows films pertaining to significant moments in Jewish history and the Jewish experience, portrayed in movies, TV and theatre. Visit George Segal's poignant sculpture "The Holocaust" on the second floor. The museum carries an atmosphere of devotion seldom felt in other museums. The writer urges you to visit the Jewish Museum.

METROPOLITAN MUSEUM OF ART

OPEN:	*Wed-Sun 9:30-5:15*	ADD:	*5th Ave @ 82 St*
	Tues 9:30-8:45	TEL:	*212-879-5500*
CLOSED:	*Mon & Holidays,*	TYPE:	*Fine Arts*
	Thanksgiving, Christmas,	ENTRY:	*Adult $5*
	New Years Day		*Sr & Stud $2.50*
SUB:	*IRT Lex to 86 St*	RATING:	****
BUS:	*Mad Ave to 82 St*		

It would be impossible to cite all that the Magnificent Met offers. The number of books written on it could fill a large library. It's one of the most celebrated institutions of art in the world, certainly the largest in the country with dozens of separate sections, each one more astonishing than the next. Its collection is so vast that only a small fraction can be displayed at one time. Everything you ever dreamed of seeing under one roof is here. It's simply mind-boggling. Don't even think of doing the Met in one day; you couldn't cover everything in six months. To give you an idea of the complexity and expense of running this massive operation, the Met staffs nearly 2,000 employees and budgets roughly $85 million a year. It also offers ten different types of membership plans. There are 32 acres of floor space and 21 separate gift shops. Notice upon entering that each section has its own hours. If you plan on more than one visit, I strongly advise having a game plan for each attack. If not, it's curtains for the equilibrium. Elevate on up to the roof garden, even briefly, for a spectacular view of New York. Lunch, brunch, or cocktails on the main floor. Don't forget the Junior Museum in the lower level. This amazing museum has proven that through intelligent planning and management, a museum can be not only self-supporting, but successfully profitable.

MUSEUM OF THE CITY OF NEW YORK

OPEN:	*Tues-Sat 10-5*	ADD:	*1220 5th Ave @ 103 St*
	Sun 1-5	TEL:	*212-534-1672*
CLOSED:	*Mon*	TYPE:	*Historical*
SUB:	*IRT Lex to 103 St*	ENTRY:	*Voluntary Donation*
BUS:	*Mad Ave to 102 St*	RATING:	***

The main focus of this museum is its collection of paintings, maps, photographs, and documents pertaining to New York from its early Dutch settlement in the early 1600s into a major American force of our time. Try to see the multi-media film "Big Apple," a 20-minute jazzy run through New York's past. Sunday walking tours of the neighborhoods of New York's five boroughs draw large crowds, so book early. It's a bargain at $10. The gift shop sells an assortment of books on the history of the five boroughs. I still can't imagine why there are two of Mr. Rockefeller's rooms on the fifth floor. On your way out, glance at the display of New York before the White Man arrived. If you've ever lived, or wanted to live in New York, no matter for how long, visit this museum.

NATIONAL ACADEMY OF DESIGN

OPEN: *Wed-Sun 12-5*	ADD: *1083 5th Ave @ 89 St*
Tues 12-8	TEL: *212-369-4880*
CLOSED: *Mon & Holidays*	TYPE: *Fine Arts*
SUB: *IRT Lex #4, 5, 6 to 86 St*	ENTRY: *Adult $2.50*
BUS: *M1, M2, M3 to 86 St*	*Sr & Stud $2*
	RATING: ****

The museum's function is threefold: it is a museum, an honorary society of artists, and a school of fine arts, all highly prestigious. The patrician townhouse has four floors filled with paintings, sculptures, drawings, arts and architecture, a grand winding staircase with Diana at its base, and elegant galleries. The museum maintains a legendary membership roster that is enviable for its major masters and distinguished designers, all of whom have submitted a self portrait and their most prized works. Aside from this permanent collection, there's a wealth of Renaissance treasures. The changing exhibitions can be described as matchless. The gift shop offers a most unusual and varied collection of art books and cards. I highly recommend the Academy: it's rarely visited, yet it's one of New York's best.

UKRAINIAN INSTITUTE

OPEN:	*Tues-Fri 2-6*	ADD:	*2 E 79 St*
	Sat, Sun by appt	TEL:	*212-288-8660*
CLOSED:	*Mon, Holidays*	TYPE:	*Ethnic*
SUB:	*IRT Lex #4, 5, 6 to 77 St*	ENTRY:	*Voluntary Donation*
BUS:	*5th or Mad to 77 St*	RATING:	***

The mansion 's striking architecture stands out along Fifth
Avenue's Museum Mile. Its multiple turrets and domes lend
the illusion of a castle lifted out of a European fairy tale.
Designed in 1900 as a private villa, purchased and renamed
in the 1950s by the Society's founder, it's recently been
designated a National Historical Landmark. The aim of the
Ukraine Society is to develop, sponsor and promote
Ukrainian activities and to acquaint the public with the
Ukraine's culture, history, art, and music through films,
concerts, lectures, and classes. It's also a research center
with archives and documents pertaining to the 20th-century
Ukraine. There's a permanent costume display and a
religious and folk art display. The Institute hosts temporary exhibitions showing prominent artists from the
Ukraine.

WHITNEY MUSEUM

OPEN:	*Wed-Sat 11-5*	ADD:	*945 Mad Ave @ 75 St*
	Tues 11-8, Sun 12-6	TEL:	*212-570-3676*
CLOSED:	*Mon, Major Holidays*	TYPE:	*Fine Arts*
SUB:	*IRT Lex #4,5,6 to 77 St*	ENTRY:	*All $4.50*
BUS:	*M1, M2, M3,*		*Free Tues Eve 6-8*
	M4 to 77 St	RATING:	****

The Whitney concentrates on the unique and extraordinary
in modern American art and remains one of the world's
foremost centers for 20th century art. Gertrude Vanderbilt
Whitney, a sculptress and art collector, created the museum
in 1930, and the majority of the permanent collection
consists of her acquisitions. Changing exhibitions and
special events are first-class and educational programs are
more than successful. The permanent collection soars in its
greatness. For some reason the restaurant enjoys immense
popularity. Odd for a museum, but perhaps the food is just
plain good. Whitney has three public branch museums:
Equitable Center, 7th and 51st; Philip Morris Center, 42nd
and Park; and Federal Reserve Plaza, Maiden Lane. All are
free and superb. You get more than your money's worth at
Whitney.

UPTOWN WEST

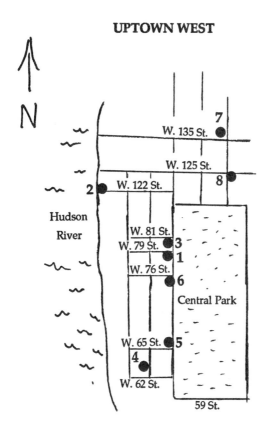

1. AMERICAN MUSEUM OF NATURAL HISTORY
2. GENERAL GRANT TOMB
3. HAYDEN PLANETARIUM
4. LINCOLN CENTER
5. MUSEUM OF AMERICAN FOLK ART
6. NEW YORK HISTORICAL SOCIETY
7. SCHOMBERG CENTER
8. STUDIO MUSEUM IN HARLEM

AMERICAN MUSEUM OF NATURAL HISTORY

OPEN:	*Mon, Tues, Thur, Sun 10-6*	ADD:	*Cntral Pk West @ 79 St*
	Wed, Fri, Sat 10-9	TEL:	*212-769-5920*
CLOSED:	*Thanksgiving, Christmas,*	TYPE:	*Science*
	New Years	ENTRY:	*Suggested Adult $3.50*
SUB:	*IND C or K to 81 St*		*Sr & Stud $1.50*
BUS:	*M7, M10 to 81 St*		*Free Fri & Sat evenings*
		RATING:	****

The museum, the largest of its kind in the world, occupies four city blocks and 22 buildings, with an incredible range of objects in natural sciences, anthropology, biology, paleontology, zoology, and mineralogy. To avoid being overwhelmed pick up a free brochure at the entrance, think about the subject you prefer, and take the plunge. Keep your plan as simple as possible. I reccommend the Akeley Hall of African Mammals, main floor; The Hall of Ocean Life, main floor; and The Halls of Early and Late Dinosaurs, fourth floor. Or, drop into the NatureMax Theatre, main floor, for The Earth and Its Creatures, a film with explosive impact. One shortcoming, however, is the need for improved lighting in the older, more remote sections. Nevertheless it's the best natural history show in town and a must on your museum itinerary.

GENERAL GRANT'S TOMB

OPEN: *Wed-Sun 9-5*	ADD: *Riverside Dr. @ 122 St*
CLOSED: *Mon,Tues & Nat'l Hol*	TEL: *212-666-1640*
SUB: *IRT #1 to 116 St*	TYPE: *Historical*
BUS: *5th Ave to 116 St*	ENTRY: *Voluntary Donation*
	RATING: **

Ulysses S. Grant, Civil War hero and two-term President of the United States, was a rather quiet man and not widely understood. Grant was so admired by the Black community that in 1868 it was that group which decided his election to the presidency. The museum is his mausoleum, fashioned after Napoleon's tomb in Paris. Grant's life is portrayed in photographs, portraits, documents and drawings. Notice that one of his close friends was Mark Twain. The three immense mosaic murals show Grant as the central figure in three major Civil War battles: Vicksburg, Chattanooga, and Appomattox. After his presidency, he and his wife received international acclaim on a worldwide goodwill tour. Grant at his death was a mere 63 years old, leaving behind not only an illustrious career, but a monumental work, his personal memoirs.

HAYDEN PLANETARIUM

OPEN: *Mon-Fri 12:30-4:45*	ADD: *81 St @ Cntrl Park West*
CLOSED: *Thanksgiving, Christmas*	TEL: *212-769-5920*
SUB: *IND C, K to 81 St*	TYPE: *Science*
BUS: *M7, M 10 to 81 St*	ENTRY: *Adult $3.75*
	Sr & Stud $2.75
	RATING: ****

Have you ever wondered why the sky is blue? Or what makes a rainbow? Well, the solutions are found here, along with many other answers about heavenly phenomena and wonders of the universe. This is actually the astronomy department of the Museum of Natural History. The star attraction is upstairs in the Sky Theater with a huge domed ceiling and chairs that recline to almost lying position - the better to see the star-studded show. The Hall of the Sun, also upstairs, has exhibits about that most perplexing celestial body, the Sun. The Guggenheim Theater on the main floor shows films with vivid sound effects in its 360° room. There are exhibits on astronomy, space science, the moon, the planets, extraterrestrial life, meteors, minerals, and gems. Be prepared for groups of children, and you know what that means.

LINCOLN CENTER FOR THE PERFORMING ARTS

OPEN: *Museum-Mon, Tues,*	ADD: *B'way @ 65 St*
Thurs 10-8, Wed-Fri 12-6	TEL: *212-877-1800*
Sat 10-6	TYPE: *Miscellaneous*
CLOSED: *Museum-Sun*	ENTRY: *Free*
*Lincoln Center	RATING: ****
Complex is Open Year-Round Daily	

Because music, theater and dance are part of the Arts, and because Lincoln Center is dedicated to the perpetuation of higher forms of art, I've included this stunning complex, completed in 1969, as a significant chapter in the Museums of New York. The architectural design alone is a sight to behold. There are six buildings: New York State Theater, Metropolitan Opera House, Juilliard School and Alice Tully Hall, Vivian Beaumont Theater, Public Library and Museum of the Performing Arts, and Avery Fisher Hall. Although each conducts its own programs and activities, all operate closely to and with one another. Broadcasts, telecasts, festivals, competitions, and community programs share the common interest of fine arts. Future plans for an ambitious enlargement program will increase Lincoln Center's space in a 25-story building. Take a one-hour guided tour, and as long as you're here, stop in at the extraordinary Museum of the Performing Arts. I promise you no regrets.

MUSEUM OF AMERICAN FOLK ART

OPEN: *Daily Year-Round*	ADD: *2 Lincoln Square @*
CLOSED: *Major Holidays*	*Columbus Ave & 65 St*
SUB: *IRT 7th Ave #1, 2, 3 to*	TEL: *212-481-3080*
66 St Lincoln Center	TYPE: *General*
	ENTRY: *Free*
	RATING: ****

This is a branch of the main museum and will remain here as interim headquarters. Its permanent home on West 53 Street is scheduled for reopening in the early 1990s. This branch's structural design is unusual: four wings radiate from a central sky-lit atrium and garden court. This public area serves as a backdrop for the large-scale enchanting folk sculptures. Each year four exhibitions of folk art are held with an occasional one-man show. Devotees of American Folk Art are ecstatic about the long overdue recognition of their beloved artistry. There is a refreshing charm and universal appeal here. Naive art is truly a welcome respite from today's tense, high-tech pace. Stop in at the gift shop just next door for books and one-of-a-kind handcrafted items. Call first: this museum may not open until the winter of 1989.

NEW YORK HISTORICAL SOCIETY

OPEN:	*Tues-Sat 10-5*	ADD:	*170 Central Pk West*
	Sun 1-5	TEL:	*212-873-3400*
CLOSED:	*Mon & Major Holidays*	TYPE:	*Historical*
SUB:	*IND B, C, K to 81 St*	ENTRY:	*Adult $2*
BUS:	*M7, M10, M11 to 76 St*		*Sr & Stud $1.50*
		RATING:	***

A word must be said about this 19th-century Beaux Arts granite building: it's an austere reminder of yesterday's grand, then upper west side of New York. As its name implies, the Society concerns itself with all facets of Americana, with emphasis on New York. It's a combination museum and research library. Special attractions are the Silver Gallery, James Audubon watercolor illustrations, 17th- and 18th- century period rooms, and a glittering display of Tiffany glass and lamps. The upper floor holds a wealth of information on the urban and suburban landscape of New York, fine painting and portrait galleries, and a library with priceless manuscripts, documents, and books. This is a treasure house. You might glimpse at the wall map of the British Empire in America, c. 1733. The museum store must be visited. Everything you always wanted to know about New York is here and in style.

SCHOMBERG CENTER FOR RESEARCH IN BLACK CULTURE

OPEN: *Mon, Wed 12-8*	ADD: *515 Lenox @ 135 St*
Thurs, Fri, Sat 10-6	TEL: *212-862-4000*
CLOSED: *Sun, Tues*	TYPE: *Ethnic*
SUB: *IRT 7th Ave #2, 3 to 135 St*	ENTRY: *Free*
BUS: *M7, M100, M101 to 135 St*	RATING: *****

This is an important research center of the New York Public Library with reference rooms, archives, and large galleries. It was founded by Arthur Schomberg, a Puerto Rican of African descent. The Center contains about a million volumes by or about Africans and Afro-Americans, in addition to periodicals, pamphlets, manuscripts, prints and drawings, photographs, paintings, sculpture, sheet music, recorded music, posters, and playbills. It's the world's most comprehensive documentation of Blacks and extremely thought- provoking, enormously rich in history, folklore, and the roots of the Black experience. Located in the heart of Harlem, the library is a reminder of a spiritual legacy handed down to us by generations of a wounded community.

STUDIO MUSEUM IN HARLEM

OPEN:	*Wed-Fri 10-5*	ADD:	*144 West 125 St*
	Sat, Sun 1-6	TEL:	*212-864-4500*
CLOSED:	*Mon, Tues*	TYPE:	*Ethnic*
SUB:	*IRT 7th Ave #2,*	ENTRY:	*Adult $1.50*
	3, to 125 St		*Sr & Stud $.50*
BUS:	*M2, M7, M100 to 125 St*	RATING:	***

This excellent museum is devoted solely to African, Afro-American and Caribbean artists and is home to treasures of black art and artifacts. It opened during the height of the Civil Rights movement in 1968 and has grown and developed into an elegant, sophisticated cultural institution. The permanent collection of paintings, prints, sculptures, weaving, and photographs is superior. Changing exhibits present arts of Black America and the African diaspora through the eyes and hands of eminent artists. Workshops, tours, films, educational programs, seminars, and classes are held here, as is an artist-in-residence program. The historic photographic essay of Harlem in its heyday by James Van Der Zee shouldn't be missed. The museum's goal for a sculpture garden is close to fulfillment. It's on the way to becoming one of the world's leading art centers.

WASHINGTON HEIGHTS

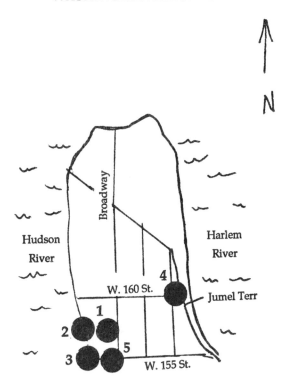

1. AMERICAN ACADEMY OF ARTS AND LETTERS
2. AMERICAN NUMISMATIC SOCIETY
3. HISPANIC SOCIETY
4. MORRIS-JUMEL MANSION
5. MUSEUM OF THE AMERICAN INDIAN

AMERICAN ACADEMY OF ARTS AND LETTERS

OPEN:	*Tues-Sun 1-4 Exhibitions Only*	ADD:	*Audubon Terr.*
	March, May/June, Nov/Dec	TEL:	*368-5900*
	Broadway & 155 St	TYPE:	*Miscellaneous*
SUB	*#1 IRT to 157 St & B"way*	ENTRY:	*Free*
BUS:	*M4, M5, to 156 St*	RATING:	***

The Academy is an organization formed for the recognition of persons of special distinction in literature and the arts, architecture, poetry, music, and a dozen or more recipients of fellowships and memorial awards. Membership in the Academy consists of eminent artists, musicians, and writers from both the United States and foreign countries. The membership list is more than impressive, and to be invited to join the Academy is considered recognition of the highest artistic merit. Three exhibitions a year are held during March, May/June, and November/December. The galleries are open to the public only during those times and visitors must call first. The Academy is housed in two buildings with elegant appointments and fine paintings, appropriate to this particular component of artistic aristocracy. Although the neighborhood is not attractive, it might behoove you to make the trip.

AMERICAN NUMISMATIC SOCIETY

OPEN:	*Tues-Sat 9-4:30*	ADD:	*Audubon Terrace*
	Sun 1-4		*B'way @ 155 St*
CLOSED:	*Mon*	TEL:	*212-234-3130*
SUB:	*B'way #1 to*	TYPE:	*Miscellaneous*
	157 St B'way	ENTRY:	*Free*
BUS:	*M4, M5 to 156 St*	RATING:	**

Numismatics is the study of coins, currency, and medals as they relate to history, archeology, and economics. The museum is composed of two rooms. The first tells the story of the development of coins from BC until today. The second is devoted to decorations and medals of honor covering the broad expanse of thousands of years and dozens of countries, and includes commemorative coins of historic events. Not only is their library endowed with a comprehensive collection of periodicals and catalogs, but there is a large segment of serious students and collectors who maintain diligent interest in the Society. A scholarliness prevails throughout. The study of coinage is yet another means to a broader understanding of the origins and nature of civilizations before our own. To enter, ring the bell for a guard.

HISPANIC SOCIETY OF AMERICA

OPEN:	*Tues-Sat 10-4:30*	ADD:	*Audubon Terrace*
	Sun 1-4		*B'way @ 155 St*
CLOSED:	*Mon, Holidays*	TEL:	*212-926-2234*
SUB:	*B'way #1 to*	TYPE:	*Ethnic*
	157th & B'way	ENTRY:	*Voluntary Contribution*
BUS:	*M4, M5 to 156 St*	RATING:	**

One might imagine imagine that the word Hispanic would suggest a presentation of present-day social conditions. This, however, is not the case. All contents pertain to Iberian (Spanish/Portuguese) literature, sculpture, paintings, ceramics, and decorative arts dating from Roman/ Moorish civilizations. After entering, go up to the first floor. The main gallery with its high ceiling and balcony overlooking a solemn two-story salon encircled by sculptured archways is truly grand. Early Mediterranean arts and hand-set mosaic portions of rooms are voluptuous. The only problem is that not all exhibits are dated. The viewer is therefore left to his own devices. The library holds thousands of volumes, maps, and historic manuscripts. Did you notice the Hebrew Bible? Top off your visit with a glance at the El Greco, Goya, and Velasquez paintings.

MORRIS-JUMEL MANSION

OPEN:	*Tues-Sun 10-4*	ADD:	*1765 Jumel Terrace*
CLOSED:	*Mon, All Holidays*	TEL:	*212-923-8008*
SUB:	*IND A to 125 St,*	TYPE:	*Historical*
	local B to 163 St	ENTRY:	*Adult $2*
BUS:	*#2, 3, Madison Ave to*		*Sr & Stud $1*
	St. Nicholas & 160 St	RATING:	**

Not only is this Georgian residence situated atop the highest spot in New York City, but it is one of only a half-dozen mansion/villa museums remaining from the 17th to the 19th centuries (Abigail Adams and Teddy Roosevelt's residences are two others). The museum holds some great historic memories. Firstly, Aaron Burr was married here to Mme Jumel. Secondly, the mansion's claim to having served briefly as George Washington's headquarters in 1776 is perfectly true. In addition, the villa was used during the 1780s as military governing chambers. Federal/Empire period furnishings are intact; charming flowered wallpaper is in some rooms, Napoleonic design in others; and the octagonal drawing room is tastefully elegant. What a pleasure to visit one of the last vestiges of Old New York!

MUSEUM OF THE AMERICAN INDIAN

OPEN:	*Tues-Sat 10-5*	ADD:	*Audubon Terrace*
	Sun 1-5		*B'way @ 155 St*
CLOSED:	*Mon*	TEL:	*212-283-2420*
SUB:	*B'way #1 to 157*	TYPE:	*Ethnic*
	St & B'way	ENTRY:	*Adult $3*
BUS:	*M4, M5 to 156 St*		*Sr & Stud $2*
			Native American Free
		RATING:	***

The three story museum has more than four million artifacts representing Native American culture of the western hemisphere. Names like Seminole, Navajo, Iroquois, Cherokee, Sitting Bull, Crazy Horse and Geronimo are scattered about like jewels in a sea of beads and wampum. Masks (false faces) and clothing, pottery and sculpture, superstitious images and spiritual animals, paintings and prints, and the crafts are treasures one and all. We have George Heye to thank for all this, the compulsive accumulator, who, at the turn of this century, swept through the Americas buying anything and everything he could fasten his acquisitive hands and money on, enabling us to celebrate the American Indian's influence on our civilization. The museum needs more space, and rumor has it that a decision to move is imminent.

INWOOD

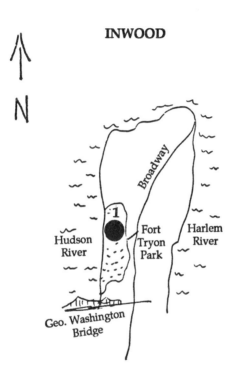

1. THE CLOISTERS

THE CLOISTERS

OPEN:	*Tues-Sun 9:30-5:15 Mar-Oct*	ADD:	*Fort Tryon Park*
	9:30-4:45 Nov-Feb	TEL:	*212-923-3700*
CLOSED:	*Mons & Holidays*	TYPE:	*Fine Arts*
SUB:	*IND 8th to 190 St*	ENTRY:	*Voluntary Contri.*
BUS:	*M4 to Cloisters*	RATING:	****

The Cloisters, an ecclesiastical setting high above the Hudson River at the north tip of Manhattan, is more than tranquil: it is ephemeral and immortal. Several medieval Romanesque and Gothic cloisters, monasteries and gardens are all faithfully presented. The newly- designed Treasury holds a spectacular collection of precious works of art, textiles, woods and ivories, liturgical objects, and gold and enameled pieces. Another treasure is the Unicorn Tapestries, similar to those in the Musee de Cluny in Paris. Chapels hold paintings and altarpieces: galleries hold manuscripts, sculptures and stained glass panels. Flower and herb gardens are of lovely simplicity. The Cloisters, a branch of the Metropolitam Museun of Art, provides a scholarly and beautiful glimpse back into the Middle Ages. On weekends during the summer shuttle bus trips are offered from the Met.

1. AMERICAN MUSEUM OF THE MOVING IMAGE
2. BOWNE HOUSE
3. HALL OF SCIENCE
4. KINGSLAND HOUSE
5. NOGUCHI MUSEUM AND GARDENS
6. QUEENS BOTANICAL GARDEN
7. QUEENS MUSEUM

AMERICAN MUSEUM OF THE MOVING IMAGE

OPEN:	*Wed & Thurs 1-5*	**ADD:** *35 Ave @ 36 St Astoria*
	Fri 1-9 , Sat 10-9	**TEL:** *718-784-0077*
	Sun 10-5	**TYPE:** *Media*
CLOSED:	*Mon & Tues*	**ENTRY:** *Adult $4*
SUB:	*B'way R or IND G to*	*Sr & Stud $2*
	Steinway St. Astoria	**RATING:** ****

This museum is one of the most complex centers of art in New York. It's a gigantic attempt at demystifying mass entertainment and conveying TV and video's magic and impact on our culture and society. Why Queens? Well, Astoria enjoys the privilege of having been a major center for the entire East Coast during the heyday of film- making. Their presentations are close to perfection, their galleries are huge, and the movie theater will set you spinning. Nothing is left to chance. Their technical displays are intricate and mind boggling. Demonstrations of the moving image are fast paced and very visual. You could spend the entire day here and still not experience everything. The museum has established itself as a world-class exhibition center. Its setting is highly eclectic and inventive. Don't miss the Enchanted Mirror (second floor). On the way out, visit the extraordinary gift shop.

BOWNE HOUSE

OPEN: *Tues, Sat, Sun 2:30-4:30*	ADD: *3701 Bowne St, Flushing*
CLOSED: *Mid Dec to Mid Jan*	TEL: *718-359-0528*
SUB: *IRT #7 to Main St*	TYPE: *Historical*
Flushing	ENTRY: *Adult $1*
LIRR to Flushing	*Child .25*
	RATING: ***

John Bowne built this house in 1660 and it's probably the oldest building in New York. Its significance is not confined to its architectural quality, however, for it carries a more spiritual connotation. At that time Governor Peter Stuyvesant outlawed any and all religions not of the Dutch Church. Mr. Bowne, a Quaker, held meetings for worship, was arrested, imprisoned and banished to Europe for two years, then returned to his family in Flushing. It is felt that as a direct result of this drama the gentle, modest Quakers were granted religious freedom, which eventually led to the adoption of the Constitution's First Amendment a century later. Thanks to successive Bowne generations and the Bowne Historical Society, Bowne House retains all its original furnishings and touching simplicity.

HALL OF SCIENCE

OPEN: *Wed-Sun 10-5*	ADD: *47-01 111 St Flushing Medows*
CLOSED: *Mon, Tues*	TEL: *718-699-0675*
SUB: *IRT #7 to 111 St*	TYPE: *Science*
	ENTRY: *Adult $2.50*
	Sr & Stud $1.50
	RATING: ***

The Hall of Science is a science-technology center created by the San Francisco Exploratorium and funded by IBM, and it's a smash hit. Based on the premise that science is more fascinating with the help of human participation, all exhibits encompass and connect everyday reflexes like hearing, motion, balance, and common sense to scientific phenomena with hands-on help. The museum is on the lower level. The upper portion is hollow, 80 feet high, of curved cement, with its walls inlaid in blue stained glass, and viewed from the inside it's pretty dazzling. The building's odd configuration was done for the 1964 World's Fair, by the very same architect who designed the Trylon and Perisphere for the 1939 World's Fair. The museum is crowded with visitors at all times and the excitement (noise) level is very high.

KINGSLAND HOUSE

OPEN:	*Tues, Sat Sun 2:30-4:30*	ADD:	*143-55 37th Ave Flushing*
CLOSED:	*Mon, Wed, Thurs, Fri,*	TEL:	*718-939-0647*
	Christmas, N. Years Day	TYPE:	*Historical*
SUB:	*IRT #7 to Main St*	ENTRY:	*Voluntary Donation*
LIRR:	*to Flushing*	RATING:	***

Although Kingsland Homestead was built by a wealthy Quaker farmer named Doughty, it derives its name from an English sea captain, Joseph King, who married Doughty's daughter and inherited the house. Its architecture is in Revolutionary-Dutch-English style, with typically quadrant windows, gambrel roof, and central chimney. Kingsland House features changing Victorian exhibitions. The Queens Historical Society's quarters are upstairs and it is they who, along with the Kingsland Preservation Committee, plan workshops, lectures, and historical exhibitions. On permanent display are Captain King's documents and rare books, photos of early Queens, and maps dating back to the mid-1850s. That enormous beech tree alongside the building, the oldest of its kind in the US, was planted around 1850 and is still growing.

NOGUCHI MUSEUM AND GARDENS

OPEN:	Wed & Sat 12-5 April-Nov	ADD:	32-37 Vernon Blvd @ 33rd Rd Astoria
		TEL:	718-204-7088
SUB:	BMT RR Astoria to B'way	TYPE:	Fine Arts
		ENTRY:	Suggested Donation $2
		RATING:	***

It's nice to see an artist given the achnowledgments due him. Isamu Noguchi is considered a pure, innovative artist. His museum and gardens occupy a small triangular city block just under the 59th Street Queensborough Bridge on the Queens side. His works are intermingled within the museum's twelve galleries, each differing in style and material, but all sparkling with imposing power. Outside, his more recent chiseled granite boulders grace the gardens dotted with bird baths and gurgling water basins. Although his models are not visible, Noguchi has designed stage settings for the Martha Graham Dance Company, and created sculptural pieces for Rockefeller Center in New York, a memorial bridge for Hiroshima, a fountain on Fifth Avenue, a park in Miami, a marble sculpture for Venice, and more. There's a calming influence here. Noguchi's simplicity glows.

QUEENS BOTANICAL GARDENS

OPEN: *Daily Year-Round*
8-dusk
SUB: *IRT #7 to Main St*
Transfer to Q44
to Gardens

ADD: *43-50 Main St Flushing*
TEL: *718-886-3800*
TYPE: *Botanical*
ENTRY: *Free*
RATING: ***

Here's a bit of the country amid the clatter, clamor, and congestion of Flushing. Created only 25 years ago, these gardens are proof that it is possible to enjoy a variety of foliage without leaving town. Individual gardens are harmoniously designed, and tiny walks lead to tinkling waterfalls and rocky grottoes. There's a Bird Garden, an Herb Garden, a Bee Garden, a Fountain Garden, and, of course, a Rose Garden. The Victorian Wedding Garden is reserved for ceremonies and photographs. The most desirable time of year to visit is the Fall, when foliage is at its peak with blazing scarlets and yellows. It's not the largest botanical garden in New York, but one can sit on any bench and do nothing but admire flora and fauna and listen to birds.

QUEENS MUSEUM

OPEN: *Tues-Fri 10-5*	ADD: *NYC Bldg. Flushing Mdws*
Sat & Sun 12-5:30	TEL: *718-592-2403*
CLOSED: *Mon*	TYPE: *Fine Arts*
SUB: *IRT #7 to Willets Pt*	ENTRY: *Adult $2*
BUS: *Q48 to Willets Pt*	*Sr & Stud $1*
	RATING: ***

The building was constructed to house the New York City
Exhibit for the 1939 World's Fair. You can't miss it: it's just
next door to the Unisphere. Between then and now it has
hosted the UN General Assembly (1946-50) and the second
World's Fair in 1964. On permanent display is "The Heroic
Spirit," a stunning sculpture gallery. Another attraction is
"Panorama," a scale model of New York's five boroughs.
Temporary exhibitions range from early to contemporary
arts. Visit the sculpture restoration studio in the basement.
If you're lucky enough to be at this museum at the right
time you might catch the Tennis Open next door, a New
York Mets ball game across the lawn, or both. Also, weather
permitting, you're directly under the take-off pattern for La
Guardia airport, an added attraction.

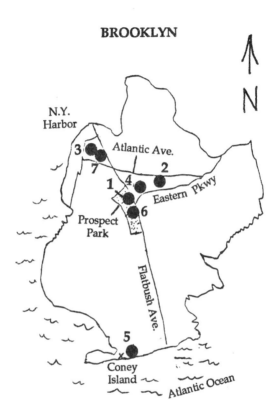

1. BROOKLYN BOTANICAL GARDENS
2. BROOKLYN CHILDREN'S MUSEUM
3. BROOKLYN HISTORICAL SOCIETY
4. BROOKLYN MUSEUM
5. NEW YORK AQUARIUM
6. PROSPECT PARK ZOO
7. TRANSIT AUTHORITY MUSEUM

BROOKLYN BOTANICAL GARDENS

OPEN:	*Summer: Tues-Fri 8-6*	ADD:	*1000 Washington Ave*
	Holidays & Wknds 10-6	TEL:	*718-622-4433*
	Winter: Tues-Fri 8-4:30	TYPE:	*Gardens*
	Hol & Wknds 10-4:30	ENTRY:	*Voluntary Contribution*
CLOSED:	*Mon*	RATING:	****
SUB:	*IRT 7th #2,3 to Eastern Pkwy*		

The elegant Botanical Gardens, whose slogan is "many gardens within a garden", lives up to its reputation. Pick up a small booklet at the entrance for a complete diagram of the gardens. The new Steinhardt Conservatory with a $2 admission charge is worth every penny. It's a vision in superb glass architecture with three separate pavilions in delicately tinted glass with a bonsai museum at one end, an aquatic greenhouse at the other, and a number of remarkable collections in between. There are roughly 25 individual gardens including the Cranford Rose Garden, the Shakespeare Garden, the English Cottage Garden, the Herb Garden, and a Fragrance Garden for the blind with Braille labels. The lily ponds, luscious trees, and rolling lawns contribute to a magical beauty equalling the grandeur of Monet's gardens in Giverny. The Brooklyn Museum is just next door.

BROOKLYN CHILDREN'S MUSEUM

OPEN: *Mon,Wed,Fri 2-5*	ADD: *145 Brooklyn Ave*
Sat, Sun Holidays 10-5	TEL: *718-735-4400*
CLOSED: *Tuesday*	TYPE: *Childrens*
SUB: *IRT #3 to Kingston-*	ENTRY: *Adult #2*
Eastern Pkwy	*Sr, Stud & Child $1*
BUS: *B7, B44, B47 to Museum*	RATING: ***

This unorthodox, imaginative museum is supposed to be participatory for kids, but from the corner of my eye at more than one exhibit I caught a glimpse of several adults with their hands on. It's a high- tech, gaily painted playground, and each presentation is smartly separated from the next so as not to confuse. Upon entering, there's a stream within a "people tube," a wide drainage pipe that runs down the four levels of the museum, lit up in glorious fluorescent colors. Each level demonstrates the mysteries of the world: sounds, weights and measures, balance, artifacts, distance imagery, abstract theories, and musical impressions. Every exhibit is buoyant and dynamic. Those loud noises that you hear erupting are screams of pure pleasure. The Brooklyn Children's Museum is delightful from the moment you arrive. Transportation is complicated, so call first.

BROOKLYN HISTORICAL SOCIETY

OPEN:	*Tues-Sat 10-5*	ADD:	*128 Pierrepont St*
	Library Open 10-4:45	TEL:	*718-624-0890*
CLOSED:	*Sun, Mon*	TYPE:	*Historical*
SUB:	*IRT #2,3,4 to*	ENTRY:	*Voluntary Contribution*
	Borough Hall	RATING:	*****
BUS:	*B25, B38, B41 to Borough Hall*		

First of all, the museum building is one of Brooklyn's
architectural treasures. Secondly, there are five major
claims to fame in this borough: The Dodgers, Coney Island,
the Brooklyn Bridge, the Navy Yard and Brooklynites—all
here in photos at the Schellens Gallery. Climb the broad
staircase to the upstairs library, richly paneled in dark
woods, the epitome of research libraries. Scholars fill the
room seeking data on early Brooklyn, scanning manuscripts,
studying genealogy, or reading periodicals. The permanent
exhibits downstairs range from a photographic portrayal of
Brooklyn's Italian festivals to memorabilia of the Navy Yard
to the set from the kitchen of TV's "The Honeymooners."
Be certain to notice the photos in tribute to the Dodger fans
who, 35 years later, remain undyingly faithful to their
"Bums" in spite of their unforgivable departure to Los
Angeles. Even if you aren't from Brooklyn, you've got to
enjoy this visit.

BROOKLYN MUSEUM

OPEN:	*Wed-Mon 10-5*	ADD:	*200 Eastern Parkway*
CLOSED:	*Tues, Thanksgiving,*	TEL:	*718-638-5000*
	Christmas, Borough Hall	TYPE:	*Fine Arts*
	Borough Hall	ENTRY:	*Suggested Contribution*
SUB:	*IRT #2,3 to Eastern*		*Adult $3*
	Parkway		*Sr & Stud $1.50*
		RATING:	****

Five thousand years of culture await you at the Brooklyn
Museum, which, believe it or not, opened its doors in 1877.
Aside from having one of the most celebrated collections of
Egyptian art in the country, the period rooms are spectacular, as are the American folk art, the Oriental arts, the Print
and Drawing gallery, and the rotating exhibitions. Visit
Rodin on the fifth floor, along with Sargent's watercolors,
the Impressionist collection, the American paintings, and
some gorgeous sculptures. The museum is spacious and
clean, the artworks beautifully displayed. Nevertheless, it is
hardly visited. The museum shop is crammed full of
anything and everything: art, books, clothing and kitchen-
ware. Hear jazz on summer Sunday afternoons. And a
special children's gift shop - what a treat! This is one of
New York's better museums.

NEW YORK AQUARIUM

OPEN:	*Daily 10-5*	ADD:	*Surf Ave @ 8 St*
	Holidays & Summer	TEL:	*718-266-8711*
	Wknds 10-6	TYPE:	*Aquarium*
SUB:	*IND F,D To Coney Island*	ENTRY:	*Adult $3.75*
BUS:	*B36, B68 to Coney Island*		*Sr & Stud $1.50*
		RATING:	***

Aside from a few scattered hot dog stands and tacky tourist shops along the boardwalk, this is one of the few attractions remaining in the once legendary Coney Island. It's also the only aquarium of its kind in the New York area. The fish and marine life are from all of the world's oceans. The main attraction here is the underwater tank of beluga whales, but there are several sharks, dolphins, sea lions, a number of penguins and some giant turtles. Did you know that the turtle has survived in the sea for seven million years? All displays are clearly presented. A rare tropical fish collection is shown in one of the indoor tank buildings, along with hundreds of mysterious inhabitants of the sea. Aquatic events, shows and feedings are continuous. All in all they do a fine job. The aquarium is well staffed and well maintained, and a fitting assortment of novelties are in the gift shop. And you can always stroll along Coney Island's three-and-a-half miles of beachfront for a remembrance of things past.

PROSPECT PARK ZOO

OPEN: *Daily Summer ll-5*	ADD: *Flatbush Ave & Empire Blvd*
Winter ll-4:30	TEL: *718-965-6560*
	TYPE: *Zoological*
SUB: *IND D to Prospect*	ENTRY: *Free*
Park	RATING: **

As far as zoos are concerned, this is quite small; in fact, it's the smallest of New York's zoos—Central Park and Staten Island are the other two—and draws family spectators out on leisurely weekends in Prospect Park. You'll see monkeys, bears, camels, zebras, elephants, and a seal pool right at the entrance. It's not the place out-of-towners frequent, although I can't imagine why anyone would prefer a more crowded place to see members of the animal kingdom. Besides, as long as you're in the neighborhood visiting the Botanical Gardens and Brooklyn Museum, why not drop in? Be sure to telephone ahead. Restoration was begun in 1988 and may not be completed at this reading. The Lefferts Farmhouse next door, with a variety of farm animals, has been temporarily closed. When open, Lefferts can be visited summers only. Small is beautiful. This zoo certainly is.

TRANSIT AUTHORITY MUSEUM

OPEN:	*Mon-Fri 10-4*	ADD:	*Subway Entrance at*
	Some Sats 11-4		*Schermerhorn St @*
CLOSED:	*Sat, Sun*		*Boerum Pl*
SUB:	*IRT 7th Ave #2,3,4 to*	TEL:	*718-330-3060*
	Borough Hall	TYPE:	*Miscellaneous*
BUS:	*B25, B41 to*	ENTRY:	*Adult $1, Sr & Stud .50*
	Borough Hall	RATING:	***

You just won't believe, as you approach the subway
entrance, that this is a museum entrance, but it is. It's a
former subway station and one of the most fun museums in
Brooklyn. What nostalgia, with displays of early train
models, turnstiles, signals, subway maps, fragments of tile
subway art, fare collection devices, and tokens. There's a
graffiti/photographic display which brings New York's
cleanup campaign to light, so far fairly successful. Go
downstairs for a station filled with assorted vintage subway
trains just sitting there, all shined up. Look for the wooden
BMT car (c.1903), Coney Island trains, Brighton Beach trains,
Bronx trains, and trains of all eras. Signs are clear, simple,
and dated. Even if you've never ridden the subways of New
York, this museum makes a great trip.

BRONX

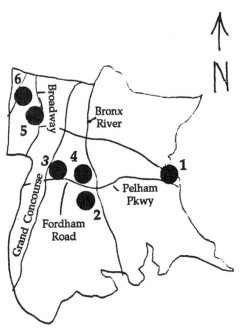

1. BARTOW-PELL MANSION
2. BRONX ZOO
3. EDGAR ALLEN POE COTTAGE
4. NEW YORK BOTANICAL GARDENS
5. VAN CORTLANDT MANOR
6. WAVE HILL CENTER

BARTOW-PELL MANSION

OPEN:	*Wed, Sat, Sun 12-4*	ADD:	*Pelham Bay Park*
CLOSED:	*Thanksgiving, Christmas,*	TEL:	*212-885-1461*
	New Years Day, Easter	TYPE:	*Historical*
SUB:	*IRT Lex #6 to*	ENTRY:	*Adult $2*
	Pelham Park		*Sr & Stud $1*
		RATING:	***

This elegant and sophisticated mansion was passed down
through generations of aristocratic and dignified Pells and
Bartows, begining in 1650. It portrays the upper-class rural
lifestyle of the Bronx in the early 1800s. The original
interior, starting with a magnificent spiral staircase, is of
supreme stateliness. Each room is designed to perfection,
mirroring the impeccable heritage of those two families.
Beautifully manicured lawns, terraces and formal gardens
top off the estate, and the lily pond is reminiscent of a
Mediterranean villa. The stone Carriage House, a ten-
minute walk from the main house, has a coach room, horse
stalls, harness room, exhibition hall, and educational center.
Its architecture alone is worth the walk. The entire setting is
austere with an intimate glimpse into the world of intimate
people.

BRONX ZOO

OPEN:	*Daily year round* *Mon-Sat 10-5:30*	**ADD:**	*Fordham Road,* *@ Bronx River Pkwy*
SUB:	*IRT B'way to Pelham* *Pkwy*	**TEL:**	*212-367-1010*
BUS:	*Liberty Exp* *@ Mad Ave & 54 St*	**TYPE:**	*Zoological*
		ENTRY:	*Adult $3* *Sr & Stud $1.50*
		RATING:	****

The zoo opened its gates around 1900. It would be imposssible to list all that is here because it's the largest zoological park in the country. Aside from the number of species represented, the quality of each is outstanding. If you entertain the notion of visiting every one of them, you'll need a two-week sojourn. For starters, there's the World of Birds, the World of Darkness, a South American Wildlife exhibit, a Serpent House, an African Plain, a Rare Animals Range and a Children's Zoo. The Zoo's unrivaled piece de resistance is a prized Snow Leopard collection. Take either the tractor train, the Bengali Express, or the monorail for a spin. Or how about a camel? The Zoo sponsors study programs and expeditions around the world. Bronx Zoo is open year-round. It's a major tourist attraction and is definitely not for kids only.

EDGAR ALLAN POE COTTAGE

OPEN: *Wed-Fri 9-5*	ADD: *Kingsbridge Rd &*
Sat 10-4	*Grand Concourse*
Sun 1-5	TEL: *212-881-8900*
CLOSED: *Mon, Tues*	TYPE: *Historical*
SUB: *IND D to Kingsbridge Rd*	ENTRY: *Voluntary Donation*
BUS: *Bx #1 to Kingsbridge Rd*	RATING: ***

The museum is a tiny wooden cottage built in 1812 for which one year's rent was $100. Edgar Allan Poe, our illustrious Poet Laureate, lived here for three years (1846-1849), his last years. During that time he penned some of his most magical works. "Annabel Lee" is one of those masterpieces. We know that from early childhood on up to the moment of his death Poe's life was tragic and painful, fraught with crises, illness, and melancholia. There are, in the three simply furnished rooms of this frail cottage, memorabilia, photos, an audio-visual presentation, and a guided tour for visitors. Shortly after his wife passed away, Poe died at the age of forty, unhappy, alone and unfulfilled. The small park named after Poe, with its bandshell gazebo, is a fitting front yard. Do pick up all available literature for a penetrating look at this tragic hero.

NEW YORK BOTANICAL GARDEN

OPEN:	*Year-Round Nov-Mar 8-6*	ADD:	*200 St & Southern Blvd*
	Apr-Oct 8-7	TEL:	*212-220-8700*
SUB:	*IRT #4 to Pelham Pkwy*	TYPE:	*Gardens*
	IND D to Bedford Park	ENTRY:	*Adult $1*
BUS:	*Bx M 11 to*		*Sr & Stud .50*
	Pelham Pkwy	RATING:	****

In 1890 the gardens, museum building and conservatory were begun with help from Messrs. Vanderbilt, Morgan, and Carnegie. The carefully planted flora and fauna are mind-boggling, a green oasis amidst the concrete and steel canyons of the Bronx. Head first for the Haupt Conservatory, a 90-foot-high glass rotunda visible from afar, which has become the Garden's logo. It's a Victorian Crystal Palace of eleven distinctive glass pavilions. There are a dozen different outdoor gardens, and the herbarium is a paradise for students of Anthropology. Through the center of all this runs the Bronx River, complete with its original forest, huge rocks, waterfalls, and great trees, all here since the very beginning. Stop at the Terrace Cafe for a snack, then it's across the street to the Bronx Zoo. Bring your camera.

VAN CORTLANDT MANOR

OPEN: *Daily 10-3 Year-Round*	ADD: *Van Cortlandt Park*
CLOSED: *Tues, Dec-Mar,*	TEL: *212-543-3344*
Major Holidays	TYPE: *Historical*
SUB: *7th Ave B'way #1 to*	ENTRY: *Adult $2*
last stop-Van Cort	*Sr & Stud $1*
Park	RATING: *******

The Van Cortlandt Manor is one of a group of elegant
colonial estates adopted by the Historic Hudson Valley
Society. They've committed themselves to the preservation
of America's heritage along the Hudson River from New
York City to Albany. This particular area, Van Cortlandt
Park, is called Croton-on-Hudson in the northernmost part
of the Bronx. The manor's original 1748 handmade structure
of rough stone and brick is intact; its interior design is Dutch
combined with early American; the parlor, living room,
kitchen, and dining room on the lower level are designed in
period furnishings, and of the several bedrooms upstairs,
one enjoys grand repute: George Washington really slept
there. The entire home is simple and tasteful. Our compli-
ments to The Society, which also holds year-round craft and
art demonstrations, family activities, historic programs, and
cooking classes.

WAVE HILL CENTER

OPEN:	*Mon-Fri 10-5:30*	ADD:	*250 St @ Independence*
	Wed til Dusk, Sun 10-7	TEL:	*212-549-3200*
CLOSED:	*Christmas,*	TYPE:	*Historical*
	New Years Day	ENTRY:	*Adult $2*
SUB:	*IRT 7th Ave #1 to 231 St*		*Sr & Stud $1*
	Trans. to Bus #10 or 7	RATING:	***
BUS:	*#1, 9 to 231 St, Trans to #10 or 7*		

This is more than an estate: it's an educational, scientific, and cultural institution high atop the Palisades at the northern tip of the Bronx called Riverdale. There are actually two manor houses, which at one time or another hosted a number of charismatic tenants, such as Teddy Roosevelt, Mark Twain, and Arturo Toscanini. The mission of Wave Hill is to examine and demonstrate the dynamic relationship between natural processes and human institutions such as science and art, archeology, horticulture, and forest management. In short, it's a successful environmental center. The botanical gardens and the greenhouses are close to perfection. You're also free to wander the 28 acres for a truly astonishing Hudson River view, and if the time is right, treat yourself to a summer outdoor sculpture show. All this plus a concert hall. Wave Hill is one of New York's sleepers.

STATEN ISLAND

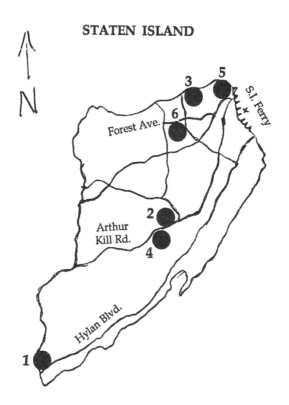

1. CONFERENCE HOUSE
2. JACQUES MARCHAIS CENTER
   OF TIBETAN ART
3. SNUG HARBOR CULTURAL CENTER
4. STATEN ISLAND HISTORICAL SOCIETY
   (RICHMONDTOWN)
5. STATEN ISLAND INSTITUTE OF ARTS AND
6. SCIENCES
7. STATEN ISLAND ZOO

CONFERENCE HOUSE

OPEN:	*Wed-Sun 1-4*	ADD:	*7455 Hylan Blvd, SI*
CLOSED:	*Mon-Tues*	TEL:	*718-984-2086*
BUS:	*SI Ferry, then*	TYPE:	*Historic*
	#103 to Hylan Blvd	ENTRY:	*Adult $1*
			Sr & Stud .50
		RATING:	***

On September 11, 1776, an important conference was held in this house. Benjamin Franklin, John Adams, and Edward Rutledge, all colonial rebels, were three of the American participants. The Other Side was represented by Admiral Lord Howe. The purpose of the conference was to attempt to stop the impending War of Independence. Despite that meeting, war was not averted. This imposing stone house has been faithfully preserved, from its facade to its interior with gracious period furnishings. By the way, this is the only pre-Revolutionary house in New York City still remaining. Be certain to go down to the basement kitchen. If you're not doing anything the first Sunday of every month, there is an authentic 18th-century cooking and baking demonstration, recipes cheerfully shared.

JACQUES MARCHAIS CENTER OF TIBETAN ART

OPEN:	*May-Sept Wed-Sun 1-5*	ADD:	*338 Lighthouse Ave SI*
	Apr, Oct, Nov Fri-Sun 1-5	TEL:	*718-987-3478*
CLOSED:	*Dec-Mar, Memorial Day,*	TYPE:	*Fine Arts*
	July 4, Labor Day	ENTRY:	*Adult $2.50*
BUS:	*SI Ferry, then #113*		*Sr & Stud $2*
	to Lighthouse Ave	RATING:	***

Jacques Marchais was really the stage name of an American woman who nurtured a passionate interest in Tibetan art. It was her sea-going grandfather who cultivated a curiosity for Southeast Asian art. He presented her with gifts which she accumulated until her marriage. Continuing on her own to enlarge her collection, she designed this Buddhist temple and filled it with these treasures. The temple is small but quite beautiful and is the largest private collection of Tibetan art in the Western world. The atmosphere is tranquil and serene; the temple brims with sensuous bronze images, paintings, silks, and samples of art from China, Nepal, India, Japan, and Southeast Asia. Her library contains thousands of volumes on Oriental philosophy, art, and history. The lotus pond and terraced gardens are total nirvana. If you are a lover of Asian culture, this visit is a must.

SNUG HARBOR CULTURAL CENTER

OPEN: *8am - midnight all year-.*
Each section of this complex
operates its own schedule

BUS: *SI Ferry, then #1 to the*
Center

ADD: *914 Richmond Terrace*
TEL: *718-448-2500*
TYPE: *Miscellaneous*
ENTRY: *Voluntary Donation*
RATING: ***

In the early 1800s this sprawling 80-acre site was built as a haven for retired seamen, and in 1976 Staten Island acquired it for use as a Cultural Center and built botanical gardens, an art center, a day-care center, a fine arts school, a maritime center, restaurants, and a children's museum. Not all the buildings have been adequately restored; however, those remaining are designed in a melange of architectural design, i.e., Greek Revival, Beaux Arts, Gothic Revival, and Italianate. Music and arts festivals, and plays are constantly going on, and if you're an aspiring artist it's possible to present a one-man (or woman) show by and for yourself. The modern and traditional sculptures scattered about are excellent. The complex is just a mile or so from the ferry. Why not spend the day?

STATEN ISLAND HISTORICAL SOCIETY
RICHMONDTOWN RESTORATION

OPEN: *Wed-Fri 10-5*	ADD: *441 Clarke Ave SI*
Sat, Sun, Mon, Hols 1-5	TEL: *718-351-1617*
	TYPE: *Historical*
BUS: *SI Ferry, then #113 to*	ENTRY: *Adult $3*
Richmond Rd	*Sr & Stud $1.50*
	RATING: ***

In 1683 Staten Island was established as a county of New York. Two hundred years later it became known as Richmondtown. Half of the 25 buildings here are open to the public. The entire mood is authentic and enjoyable. It's best to take one of the hour and a half guided tours to visit the courthouse, elementary school, and general store, and houses of the baker, basketmaker, butcher, and pottery maker. Drop by the grocery store for a bag of some of the best coffee around, and for a real chuckle have it hand ground to order by a gentleman who undoubtedly has just leapt out of a 300-year-old painting. Your receipt will be handwritten. The closest historic arena you could compare this to might be Williamsburg, Virginia. Welcome back to those lovely olden days.

STATEN ISLAND INSTITUTE OF ARTS AND SCIENCES

OPEN:	*Year-Round Tues-Sat 10-5, Sun 1-5*	ADD:	*75 Styvesant Place*
		TEL:	*718-727-1135*
CLOSED:	*Mon*	TYPE:	*Science*
BUS:	*SI Ferry, then walk to Richmond Terrace*	ENTRY:	*Adult $2*
			Sr & Stud $1
		RATING:	***

The Institute administers the Staten Island Museum, the Library and Archives, the Conservation Center, the Wildlife Refuge, the Park and Swamp. This is better than some museums and its extremely professional, housing all the arts, including decorative arts, natural sciences, fine arts, and techniques of printmaking. If you want to discover Staten Island's early history, here is the place for you to visit. And it's only three blocks from the ferry. One of the desirable features of the art portion of this museum is its sensitivity to local artists who are given as much space as the Masters. Because this is a rather small museum, the permanent exhibits have been scrupulously chosen to allow only the very best. The temporary exhibits are just as attentively offered.

STATEN ISLAND ZOO

OPEN:	*Daily Year-Round 10-4:45*	ADD:	*614 Broadway*
CLOSED:	*Thanksgiving, Christmas,*	TEL:	*718-442-3101*
	New Years Day	TYPE:	*Zoological*
BUS:	*SI Ferry, then #107 to*	ENTRY:	*Adult $1*
	Broadway		*Sr, Stud, Child Free*
		RATING:	*****

There's something about a zoo that brings families out together. Maybe it's the sharing of Mother Earth. At any rate, this one is a favorite of the Lower New York/Staten Island set. And did you know that this is New York City's biggest little zoo? Don't think that just because it's small, it doesn't have a fair variety of mammals, birds, marine and freshwater fish, and small creatures. This zoo also professes to own one of the largest and best collections of reptiles in the United States. The variety in their collection of rattle-snakes is lengthy, and I'm not certain if I've seen an assem-blage of (believe it or not) vampire bats quite like this one. The Children's Center has some charming farm animals, and it's always a delight to visit with those gracefully delicate pink flamingos.

KIDS MUSUEMS

1. STATEN ISLAND ZOO
2. STATEN ISLAND CHILDREN'S MUSEUM
3. PROSPECT PARK ZOO
4. BROOKLYN CHILDREN'S MUSEUM
5. NEW YORK AQUARIUM
6. FIREFIGHTING MUSEUM
7. CHILDREN'S MUSEUM OF MANHATTAN
8. THE MARIONETTE THEATER
9. MUSEUM OF NATURAL HISTORY/HAYDEN PLANETARIUM
10. JUNIOR MUSEUM-METROPOLITAN MUSEUM OF ART
11. AUNT LEN'S DOLL AND TOY MUSEUM
12. BRONX ZOO

KIDS MUSUEMS

KIDS MUSEUMS

Here are a number of museums designed mainly for kids.
Adults are welcome, of course. Not all those described
below have been given their own chapter in this volume.
Even though they are lesser known than their counterparts,
they are nonetheless important enough to be mentioned.
All give kids the opportunity to touch and feel exhibits, look
through microscopes, and participate in scientific discover-
ies. Notice that they are spread out across New York's five
boroughs. Consult the map on pages 94-95. The following
four museums require a telephone call in advance:

CHILDREN'S MUSEUM OF MANHATTAN
341 West 54 St   212/765-5904
Provides a setting for children to learn about art, science and
their world through participatory exhibits. Also offers a
toddler program.

STATEN ISLAND CHILDREN'S MUSEUM
Snug Harbor Cultural Center   718/273-2060
This is an innovative educational and cultural center where
children learn through hands-on exhibits.

THE MARIONETTE THEATER
16 West 61 St   212/988-9093
Located in Central Park, the museum uses puppets and
marionettes to create theater pieces with costumes, fancy sets
and music.

AUNT LEN'S DOLL AND TOY MUSEUM
6 Hamilton Terrace (141 St)   212/926-4172
Aunt Len, a retired schoolteacher, owns and operates this
entertaining museum with a collection of more than 15,000
dolls and teddy bears.

Consult the Table of Contents for the following museums:

MUSEUMS OF NEW YORK
INDEX BY TYPES

KIDS MUSEUMS

100

MUSEUMS OF NEW YORK
ALPHABETICAL INDEX

AFTERWORD

This book was designed to travel along with you. Keep it constantly at your fingertips, for it is your personal guide. Use it freely during your trip. I have provided several NOTES pages. You'll turn to them after your return for reminders of your unforgettable art experience.

I hope that, through MUSEUMS OF NEW YORK, I have provided you with rich and rewarding insights, and a finer understanding of the Arts of New York City.

To obtain ELDAN PRESS' other museum guidebooks, please use the convenient coupon below.

You will be assured of immediate delivery by ordering now.

NAME _____

ADDRESS _____

CITY _____ STATE _____ ZIP _____

I AM ENCLOSING A CHECK ($9.95 per copy plus $1 for postage and handling)

_____ Copies of MUSEUMS OF NEW YORK

_____ Copies of MUSEUMS OF PARIS

_____ Copies of MUSEUMS OF FLORENCE

_____ Copies of SMALL MUSEUMS OF THE
        FRENCH RIVIERA

ELDAN PRESS 1259 El Camino #288 Menlo Park, CA 94025

THE MUSEUMS OF NEW YORK

NOTES

NOTES

NOTES

NOTES